Indian
Astrology

Indian

Astrology

Komilla Sutton

Viking
Studio

This book is dedicated to my uncle
M. M. Singh and my brother Kuldip Wirk

Acknowledgements
I would like to thank the following for their help and support:
Marjie Neal for helping me with the manuscript; Claire Wedderburn-Maxwell and Alison
Lee for their in-house work; Emma Garner for her beautiful illustrations; Caroline
Grimshaw for designing this book; Jane Ellis for editing it; Chelsey Fox for being the best
agent; Emily and Bernard Renaud for lending me their dream cottage by the lake to write
this book; Manmeet Wirk, Ann Dilly and Diana Thayer for their loving support; Dr Ajit
Sinha for sharing his knowledge; Margaret and Jim Cahill for believing in me; and, finally,
Nani ji and Mom for being my good Karma.

VIKING STUDIO
Published by the Penguin Group
Penguin Putnam Inc., 375 Hudson Street, New York, New York 10014, U.S.A.
Penguin Books Ltd, 27 Wrights Lane, London W8 5TZ, England
Penguin Books Australia Ltd, Ringwood, Victoria, Australia
Penguin Books Canada Ltd, 10 Alcorn Avenue, Toronto, Ontario, Canada M4V 3B2
Penguin Books (N.Z.) Ltd, 182–190 Wairau Road, Auckland 10, New Zealand
Penguin Books Ltd, Registered Offices: Harmondsworth, Middlesex, England

First American edition published in 2000 by Viking Studio, a member of
Penguin Putnam Inc.

10 9 8 7 6 5 4 3 2 1

Copyright © Collins & Brown Limited, 2000
Text copyright © Komilla Sutton, 2000
Photographs copyright © see page 144.
All rights reserved

CIP data available
ISBN 0-670-89379-X

Printed and bound in Singapore; reproduction in Malaysia
Set in Fairfield
Designed by Caroline Grimshaw

Contents

Introduction

VEDIC ASTROLOGY

The ancient sages of India developed Vedic astrology over 5,000 years ago. It is part of the Vedic wisdom that includes sciences such as Ayurveda, architecture and yoga. The Vedas and the vast Vedic literature, mankind's oldest and most sophisticated body of knowledge, detail the relationships between astronomy, astrology and human beings. Indian or Vedic astrology is a path of self-knowledge, leading to harmonization of our material and spiritual needs. It helps us to find our inner light in the darkness within us, and to guide us towards our true direction.

JYOTISH, THE SCIENCE OF LIGHT

The full name of Vedic astrology is Jyotish. The word 'jyoti' has several meanings. On a practical level, it means 'a candle flame'. Symbolically, it means the light that shines down on us all from the heavens; light that gives us the ability to see through our eyes, as well as the insight to look deeper into the subtleties of life. The suffix 'sh' means 'best, wisest'. So in full, jyotish can be translated as 'the science of light' or 'the wisdom of the heavens'. Light banishes darkness; the light of knowledge dispels ignorance.

VEDIC AND WESTERN ASTROLOGY

The roots of Vedic and Western astrology are the same. Over the years Western astrology has moved in different directions, incorporating modern ideas, and has lost some of its deep philosophical base. Vedic astrology retains the deep knowledge of cosmic energy; its spiritual roots and tradition. Vedic astrology brings with it deep Eastern mysticism, philosophies, and understanding of the human spirit through the language of the stars. The roots of this language are the same but its expression becomes very different. A person who understands Western astrology will find that Vedic astrology gives a different expression of their star signs.

In Western astrology there are 12 zodiac signs from Aries to Pisces. Vedic astrology also studies the 12 signs, but further divides the zodiac into 27 different divisions or nakshatras of 13–14 days each (see the nakshatra wheel following page 17). Nakshatras are divided into three cycles of nine, which are always ruled by the planets in the same order. The nine planets are Ketu, Venus, Sun, Moon, Mars, Rahu, Jupiter, Saturn and Mercury. Vedic astrology does not use the outer planets Neptune, Uranus and Pluto.

SIDEREAL/TROPICAL ZODIACS

Vedic astrology uses a different zodiac from the one used by most western astrologers. Western astrologers use the sayana or tropical zodiac, which shows the Earth's relationship with the Sun. Indian astrologers use the nirayana, or sidereal zodiac, which is the planets' relationship with the stars. 'Sidereal' means 'of the stars'. This takes into account the celestial phenomenon known as the 'precession of the equinoxes'.

In this book, for the first time ever, I have made the calculation for you and related the sidereal position of the nakshatras to the tropical position of your Sun sign.

The Three Gunas or Psychological Qualities

'Guna' also means 'strand', the strands of twine that make up a rope. The rope is seen here as an allegory of personality. The various qualities or gunas entwine to produce the individuality of a person. The attribute of each guna is usually seen as psychological rather than physical, but the mind has a great capacity to affect the physical side of our life. Gunas play a very important part in yoga and Ayurveda. The three gunas are:

Sattva, the attribute of purity. 'Sat' means 'being, existing, pure, true and real'. 'Va' means 'where purity dwells'. A sattvic person believes in purity of being, thought, and action. Water is pure sattva. Vegetarianism is sattvic, because it rejects killing animals to fulfil the need to eat. Sattva works very much on the abstract level.

Rajas, the quality of taking action. It is the searching quality that all human beings have. It can be translated as 'pollen of the flowers', or 'emotional, moral or mental darkness'. 'Pollen of the flowers' indicates the potential of pollen to create new flowers – just as humans activate new life; experiencing life and birth. 'Moral, emotional or mental darkness' is the inability of humans to see the answers within themselves, with the result that they seek fulfilment in the material, illusionary world. Rajas moves between the abstract and the practical.

Tamas, the attribute of darkness. The Sanskrit word can also be translated as 'ignorance', making it plain that the darkness is a mental one. Tamasic people have a mental attitude that emphasizes sensuality. They can be described as lacking knowledge or spiritual insight, and enjoy a materialistic life, focusing on human sensual desires. Vedic philosophy encourages tamasic people to escape from their ignorance with the light of spiritual insight. Tamas works on the practical level.

A Sadhu, or wise man, at Amber Fort in Jaipur.

THE MEANING OF NAKSHATRAS

'Naksha' means 'to approach' and 'tra' means 'to guard'. The whole word also means 'a star'. Each nakshatra is associated with a particular star, usually the brightest in the group of stars in it. And 'nakshatra' also means 'one that never decays': the protective watch of the nakshatras over the soul will continue through many human lifetimes.

CHARACTERISTICS OF THE NAKSHATRAS

Nakshatras have their own Prakriti or individual nature. This is made up of many strands that include:
Gunas
Doshas
Aims of life

Above: The different incarnations of Vishnu.
Below right: Brahma and the Vedas (left) with a devotee of Brahma (right).

THE GUNAS ON THE THREE LEVELS OF CONSCIOUSNESS

All of us have the three gunas in our chart, but the balance between them will be different for each of us. The qualities of each nakshatra will reflect the gunas on three levels. The first level reflects your physical guna; the second level your mental quality, and the third level rules your eternal nature. The three strands of gunas intertwine to give the dominant guna of your nakshatra.

THE FOUR AIMS OF LIFE

There are four purposes in life to which each individual is born and which each of us has to experience. These are:

Dharma is correct action, our duty to others and to ourselves. It is the main thing each person should recognize: the purpose of this life. Dharma is the ability to take the right action in life, regardless of the consequences to ourselves.

Artha is the practical purpose of life, action taken with a particular, earthly purpose in mind: your work, your career, financial matters. Artha is goal-orientated.

Kama is desires and needs on a very practical level. When we are born on this earth we have to have desires. Kama is passion – sexual, religious, for life, for a cause.

Moksha is enlightenment. It means nirvana, giving up the physical life to attain higher consciousness. When we attain moksha we break away from the cycle of birth and death. Moksha is the final purpose of every incarnating soul.

DOSHAS OR WEAKNESS

The Sanskrit word 'doshas' means 'fault or weakness'. This term is used in Ayurveda, the vedic science of well being, to find the weakness in the nature of man which when aggravated causes diseases. In Indian astrology the doshas are studied to

The 27 Nakshatras

1 Ashwini – 13 to 27 April: ruled by Ketu – the South Node.
2 Bharani – 27 April to 11 May: ruled by Venus.
3 Krittika – 11 to 25 May: ruled by Sun.
4 Rohini – 25 May to 8 June: ruled by Moon.
5 Mrigasira – 8 to 21 June: ruled by Mars.
6 Ardra – 21 June to 5 July: ruled by Rahu – the North Node.
7 Punarvasu – 5 to 19 July: ruled by Jupiter.
8 Pushya – 19 July to 2 August: ruled by Saturn.
9 Ashlesha – 2 to 16 August: ruled by Mercury.
10 Magha – 16 to 30 August: ruled by Ketu.
11 Purva Phalguni – 30 August to 13 September: ruled by Venus.
12 Uttara Phalguni – 13 to 26 September: ruled by Sun.
13 Hasta – 26 September to 10 October: ruled by Moon.
14 Chitra – 10 to 23 October: ruled by Mars.
15 Swati – 23 October to 6 November: ruled by Rahu.
16 Vishakha – 6 to 19 November: ruled by Jupiter.
17 Anuradha – 19 November to 2 December: ruled by Saturn.
18 Jyeshta – 2 to 15 December: ruled by Mercury.
19 Mula – 15 to 28 December: ruled by Ketu.
20 Purva Ashadha – 28 December to 11 January: ruled by Venus.
21 Uttara Ashadha – 11 to 24 January: ruled by Sun.
22 Shravana – 24 January to 6 February: ruled by Moon.
23 Dhanishta – 6 to 19 February: ruled by Mars.
24 Shatabhishak – 19 February to 4 March: ruled by Rahu.
25 Purva Bhadra – 4 to 17 March: ruled by Jupiter.
26 Uttara Bhadra – 17 to 31 March: ruled by Saturn.
27 Revati – 31 March to 13 April: ruled by Mercury.

understand the subtle interplay of your body. A dosha can be your strength that also has the ability to become your weakness, both spiritually and physically.

Vata – Windy: the Air Quality

The natural qualities of vata are action, sensation, and enthusiasm. 'Vata' means 'wind'. Perception, enthusiasm, inspiration, communication, exercise and action are vata.

Pitta – Biliousness: the Fire Quality

Fire is required to digest. Pitta produces heat and controls the digestive system. Hunger, thirst, suppleness of body, cheerfulness, intelligence and vision are pitta.

Kapha – Phlegmatic: the Water Quality

Water is necessary for sustenance. Stability of the body, potency, strength, suppleness of joints, calmness and forbearance are kapha.

SPECIAL CONSONANTS/VOWELS

According to Vedic tradition, the first letter of your birth name is chosen from the special consonant or vowel related to your birth nakshatra. In this way, you are connected to your birth energy. Your name becomes like a mantra, and whenever someone says it, it creates an auspicious energy around you.

CUSP BIRTHS

Two nakshatras rule the days when one nakshatra ends and another starts. For example, if you were born on 27 April, you could be born in either Ashwini or Bharani. It is important to look in the cusp column to find out the exact time that the Sun moved into the nakshatra on your birth year.

If you were born at 12.30pm GMT on 27 April 1975, you will see from the cusp tables that the Sun moved into Bharani at 17.53 on your birthday. Therefore, you were born when the Sun was still in Ashwini and you should read up Ashwini nakshatra. If you do not know your time of birth, you should work out your nakshatra position from midday on your day of birth. The cusp details are at the end of the book, pages 140–144.

Philosophy

THE VEDAS

The Vedas are the root of Vedic astrology. They were written to sow the seed of a thought, which would mature into the tree of deeper understanding. The four Vedas are:

Rig-Veda teaches *gyana* – knowledge.
Yajur Veda deals with karma – action.
Sama Veda teaches *upasana* – meditation or worship.
Atharva Veda teaches on a variety of subjects.

THE UPANISHADS

'Upa' means 'near', 'ni' means 'down' and 'shad' mean 'to sit'. 'Shad' also means 'destruction' – the destruction of ignorance. Upanishad means to sit near a guru to understand the secret doctrine. The Upanishads were tales told in the mountains, around a fire at night; great sages used them to teach their listeners the mysteries of life.

There are 108 Upanishads. Eleven are considered to be particularly important: isha, kena, katha, prashna, mundaka, mandukya, taitiriya, aiteriya, chadogya, brihadaranyaka and shvetashvatara.

THE JOURNEY OF THE SOUL

Vedic philosophy believes in the concept of the transmigration of the soul. This birth is only a small part of the whole, because this lifetime is only one of a multitude of lives. Each lifetime is like one pearl in a necklace, but all the pearls have to be strung together

The incarnations of Shiva.

to make the necklace complete. The ultimate aim of the soul is to achieve moksha or enlightenment. Enlightenment is the state of eternal bliss. To achieve this, the soul has to lose its inherent purity and experience the cycles of life and death. These experiences mature the soul so that it is ready to achieve the ultimate level of consciousness where eternal happiness is possible.

Vedic astrology deals with the individual's connection with the universal. We break the connection when we are born as we take on a physical body. Our physical body will be different each time we are born as a human being, but there is a continuity of consciousness. We are only a particle of the whole consciousness, the cosmic law. When we die we go back into the universal to be reborn again. It is like the cycle of water, falling upon the earth and becoming steam; only to turn into a cloud and return again as water. With each birth we develop, so that finally we are able to break away from this cycle to achieve eternal peace.

THE SOUL AND MAYA – THE WORLD OF ILLUSION

When the soul is born in a human body it is meant to experience life, but not to think life is everything. However, many people,

The Indian god Vishnu.

especially at a younger age, do believe that life is everything and this world is our ultimate reality. In fact, the material world is known as Maya or the world of illusion. Maya will bring with it desires and needs, which we try to fulfil in our pursuit of happiness. However, the fulfilment of these desires does not bring happiness: it simply creates further desires. Soon we are caught up in a never-ending cycle of desires and despair. The illusion and the reality become confused in our minds. Indian philosophy accepts the need to fulfil our earthly desires, but it questions whether this is the only way to achieve happiness. We have to be in charge of our needs and not the other way round.

It is important to remember that the soul must experience life to be able to give it up. As we slowly start learning to shed desires and attachments, our souls begin to see a light. We start moving towards the things we are meant to move towards. Jyotish or Vedic astrology is the science of light.

THE LAW OF KARMA

The word 'karma' literally means 'action'. Every action we take in our present, past or future lives is our karma. The law of karma says that the ultimate responsibility for the quality of our life lies with us. We cannot blame others for what we are experiencing today. Our actions in the past (this life as well as previous ones) create situations that we have to face now, in the same way that actions taken today will result in situations to be faced at a later date.

THE THREE LEVELS OF KARMA

Each one of us deals with karma on three levels:

Sanchita karma is the storehouse of actions taken in our previous lives until today. The moment we act, our action becomes part of our sanchita karma. Sanchita karma is the karma we are born with, which is the sum total of the good and bad actions in previous incarnations.

Prarabdha karma is the karma that each of us has to face in this life – both the good and the bad. It is another karma that you cannot change. However much you may feel you are in charge of your life, you are only really in control of small parts of your life: you don't have any control over such events as unexpected accidents or natural disasters. Sanchita karma reflects the story of your life to date, while prarabdha karma represents the chapters you are going to experience in this lifetime. Prarabdha karma is both negative and positive.

Kriyamana karma is the most important of the three. This is the karma that we actually make of our own choice, our free will. It is the karma of choosing what to do – if we are experiencing financial difficulties, will we rob to solve our problems? Cut our expenses? Or work harder? Kriyamana karma is what you are going to do to improve the quality of this life. A great deal in Vedic astrology is about understanding this particular karma: understanding the choices we can make, stopping to think and to make the correct decisions. By doing that, we're improving our quality of life not only for now, but for the future, by not allowing the negative karmas to come forward.

The Grahas or Planets

THE IMPORTANCE OF GRAHAS OR PLANETS

'Grahas' is the Sanskrit name for planets. 'Grahas' means 'a home'; here it means the homes of celestial influence. Planets influence every aspect of life on earth: human destiny, the atmosphere, the nature of the seasons, and plant and animal life. The planetary energy influences our lives through the rulership of the nakshatras and their influence on our natal Sun, which forms part of our personality and life patterns. Planets also represent the seven levels of consciousness that are encasing the evolving soul and the universal law of time.

In Vedic astrology we use nine planets – the Sun and the Moon, Mars, Mercury, Jupiter, Venus, Saturn, Rahu and Ketu (the nodes of the Moon). Rahu and Ketu will be new planets to the students of Western astrology.

SURYA OR THE SUN
It rules Leo and the nakshatras Krittika, Uttara Phalguni and Uttara Ashadha

The Sun is the most important planet in astrology. We study the position of the Sun at birth to explain our inner being and its connection with the outer world. The Sun, by being placed in different nakshatras during the year, shines its divine light and brings the power of the nakshatra to light.

The Sun represents every aspect of our being: our eternal soul as well as the individual self. It represents both the physical and the mental self.

The Sun is known as 'Surya' in Sanskrit. The Sun is the ruler of the universe. It represents purusha, the male principle. We can call it the life force or 'prana'. Without solar energy to warm us, we would not exist. The Sun provides the gravitational pull that holds the planets and the stars together.

A stone relief carving at the thirteenth-century Sun Temple, Orissa, India.

THE MOON
It rules Cancer and the nakshatras Rohini, Hasta and Shravana

The Moon is known as 'Soma' in Sanskrit. The Moon controls nature: life and death, birth and rebirth. It is prakriti – the female regenerative principle, and it needs the purusha or the male polarity of the Sun to create life. The Sun gives life to the whole universe but the Moon gives life to Earth.

According to the Vedic stories, the nakshatras are the 27 wives of the Moon god – Soma. The Moon stays one day with each of its wives. Rohini was his favourite wife. The other wives, jealous of the Moon's infatuation with Rohini, complained to Brahma, the creator, who cursed the Moon to lose his power totally, but then let him regain it. This became waxing and waning cycles. The Moon is the significator of the mind in Vedic astrology. The myth of the Moon reflects the changing nature of the mind. As the Moon waxes and wanes, so do our thoughts and emotions. The Moon's many shades are reflected in our psyche. It can take us to the highest pinnacles of thought and give us the ability to conquer our worldly desires, but it also has the capacity to shut away light, forcing us to live in ignorance, governed by the desires and passions of animal instinct.

MANGALA OR MARS
It rules Aries and Scorpio and the nakshatras Mrigasira, Chitra and Dhanishta

Mars is represented in the Vedas as Kartika, the son of Shiva. According to the legend, only Shiva's seven-day-old son could destroy the demon Taraka who was terrorizing the world. Kamadeva, the god of love, shot an arrow of love towards Lord Shiva as he meditated, in the hope of arousing him and obtaining his semen. This succeeded and Shiva's semen was nurtured in the holy waters of the river Ganges by Krittikas till Kartika or Mars was born. When he was seven days old, Kartika destroyed the demon Taraka. This myth shows the strength and power of Mars.

Mars always represents courage, valour, immense strength and physical stamina. He has the capacity for achieving whatever goals he is set. He does not recognize danger; his duty is to defend.

Mars has a strong connection with spiritual realization and the search for truth. Mars strives towards the unattainable. Martian courage is required in plenty if we are to move towards a path of self-realization, for it is a journey into the unknown, where many obstacles and restrictions have to be faced.

BUDDHA OR MERCURY
It rules Gemini, Virgo and the nakshatras Ashlesha, Jyeshta and Revati

Mercury is known as 'Buddha' in Sanskrit. It indicates intellect. Together with the Sun and Moon, it forms the basis of life:

Atma – Buddhi – Manas. Atma, the soul, is represented by the Sun; Manas, the emotional mind, is represented by the Moon; and Buddhi, the intellectual mind, by Mercury. These three are essential requisites of consciousness.

According to Vedic myths, Mercury is the child of the Moon and Jupiter's wife, Tara. The Moon, as the God Soma, seduced Tara away from Jupiter. Tara (which means a star) became dissatisfied with Jupiter's purity and was attracted to the worldliness of Soma. Jupiter wanted her back, but Tara refused, and Jupiter threatened war. Brahma, the creator, forced Tara to go back to her husband, but she had already conceived Buddha, or Mercury, from her relationship with Soma. Buddhi means intellect and Buddha means the intellectual one. This story of Mercury's birth reflects the need for purity and godliness, represented by Tara (the wife is considered the greatest symbol of purity in India), to experience the sensuous side of the nature. The birth of Mercury or intellect happens when the pure soul comes into contact with the outside world.

Mercury is the son of the Moon. It is the rational and intellectual part of consciousness. The Moon is the sub-conscious mind; Mercury is the rational, practical, conscious mind, but it is still a fragment of total consciousness. What Mercury perceives as reality is a small part of outer manifestation.

BRIHASPATI OR JUPITER
It rules Sagittarius, Pisces and the nakshatras Punarvasu, Vishakha and Purva Bhadra

Jupiter is known as 'Brihaspati' or 'Guru' in Sanskrit. Brihaspati is the teacher of the gods in the Vedas. Jupiter guides humanity from the mirage of outer illusion to Inner Light with his knowledge and highly developed consciousness. Jupiter is intellectual in the true sense; he imparts knowledge that leads to enlightenment.

The god Jupiter rules the nakshatras Punarvasu, Vishakha and Purva Bhadra.

Jupiter represents expansion, happiness and higher knowledge. Jupiter gives material benefits to his devotees. Jupiter brings forth the fruits of past karma, providing affluence, comfort and happiness in this life.

In India, astrologers believe that Jupiter gives the capacity to face any problems that life has to throw at you. Jupiter's main concern is to provide a good material life so that you can concentrate on essential spiritual development.

SHUKRA OR VENUS
It rules Taurus, Libra and the nakshatras Bharani, Purva Phalguni and Purva Ashadha

Venus is known a 'Shukra' in Sanskrit. Venus is a male deity in the Vedas, the teacher to the Rakshashas (the demons). The demons in Vedic astrology are highly evolved souls who have lost the purpose of life. We, as humans, are mostly demonic in nature as we are looking for self-promotion and glory. Venus as the adviser of the demons is a spiritual teacher who guides the demons towards their lost soul.

Venus stands for refinement and human desires and deals with procreation and life on earth. It will give you pleasures and fulfil your desires, however outrageous they may be. The one thing Venus cannot do is to avert your karma or make you happy. In some ways the excessive materialism of Venus makes you realize that no amount of earthly trappings can bring you true happiness.

SHANI OR SATURN
It rules Capricorn, Aquarius and the nakshatras Pushya, Anuradha and Uttara Bhadra

Saturn is known as 'Shani' in Sanskrit. Saturn is the great teacher of cosmic truths, through restrictions, obstructions, frustrations, unhappiness, disillusionment, setbacks and even death. In the Vedas, Saturn is the son of the Sun and his shadow wife, Chayya. The relationship between the Sun and Saturn is a difficult one, as Saturn casts a shadow over the solar radiance.

Saturn is the planet of karmic retribution. It brings up karmic issues you have to deal with, things you cannot avoid. Saturn makes us dig deep into our inner resources in order to face these unpleasant and difficult tasks. It strips us of the sheaths that encase the soul to bring about immense psychological transformation, from which comes strength.

Rahu and Ketu

The Chayya Grahas or Shadow Planets

One of the key features of Vedic astrology is the importance given to Rahu and Ketu. They are known as chayya grahas (shadow planets). Their impact is mainly psychological. They represent the past life (Ketu) and its ability to influence the present experiences (Rahu). The correct understanding of these hidden forces allows us to move towards deeper understanding of self.

WHAT ARE RAHU AND KETU?

Rahu and Ketu are the names given to the nodes of the Moon. Rahu is the North Node and Ketu is the South Node. They are points on the ecliptic where the Moon is in alignment with the Sun and the Earth. They indicate the precise point of harmony with the three most important influences in our lives – the Sun, the Earth and the Moon. This relationship plays an important part in the enfolding of individual consciousness.

The prime importance given to Rahu and Ketu in Vedic astrology is one of its key features. They have been given the status of planets to emphasize their significance and the importance placed on eclipses. They are known as Chayya Grahas (shadow planets). They have no substance and are physically non-existent. Yet their influence is full of potency and spiritual significance. They represent polarities with a mission to churn up our lives in order to externalize the hidden potential and wisdom. In keeping with their shadowy nature, they work on a psychological level.

KARMA AND RAHU AND KETU

The role of Rahu and Ketu as karmic indicators of our lives is connected with their power to cause eclipses. The eclipses occur in the vicinity of Rahu and Ketu

An eclipse of the Sun.

during the Full Moon and the New Moon. As they symbolically eclipse the Sun (consciousness) and the Moon (the mind), they have a great part to play in darkening our perspective in order to bring forth new light. They deal with the concept of death and rebirth, transformation and regeneration.

Like the beads on a necklace, various lifetimes are joined together to form a necklace, each life being different but interconnected by an invisible thread. The invisible thread is Rahu and Ketu. The soul's journey in a particular lifetime and its connection with eternal life is indicated by Rahu and Ketu. Ketu deals with past karma and Rahu with the future.

We are born again and again to experience the pleasures and pains of earthly life until we recognize them to be the illusions that they are. On a subconscious of the Patala Loka (the underworld). Nagas in Vedic literature are not ordinary snakes, but serpents with hidden knowledge and wisdom. There was a great war between the gods and the demons for the control of the universe and at the centre of it was the ocean, which was being churned up to find hidden treasures and Amrita – the nectar of immortality. Vasuki helped the gods in their mission. He was the rope tied around the spiritual mountain Mandara, which was used as a rod by the gods to churn the ocean.

When the Amrita was found, the gods wanted to keep it for themselves as they felt that the demons would use it for the wrong purpose. Vasuki, being a demon, wanted it for personal glorification and materialistic happiness rather than universal good. (Sacrificing self for others is considered the godly impulse.) Vasuki was more intelligent than the other demons, and he was not willing to be distracted by the gods. He drank the nectar of immortality secretly. The Sun and the Moon complained to Lord Vishnu, creator of the universe, who was very angry at this deception. In anger he threw the Sudharshan Chakra at Vasuki and cut him into two. As Vasuki had drunk the Amrita, he was immortal and could not be killed. He remained in the skies as Rahu (the head) and Ketu (the lower half), a permanent reminder to the other planets (gods) of the darker side of life which we have to defeat in the pursuit of immortality. This allegory of life has to be understood.

The Moon god.

level we are afraid that if we give up these desires, we will lose out. Rahu and Ketu deal with this inner fight, the moral and the social choices we constantly have to make, and the dilemmas within us.

THE MYTHOLOGY
There are many myths and legends attached to Rahu and Ketu. The best-known one is of Rahu and Ketu as the Naga Vasuki – the ruler

A young woman offering prayers to the Hindu gods. Candles are often used in worship.

Without the help of Vasuki (Rahu and Ketu) the gods could not find the secret of immortality. In the same way we, as humans, cannot find our higher selves without understanding the lessons of Rahu and Ketu. They represent the darker side of our natures, which we need to overcome. Our inner emotions are like the ocean being churned. Within this ocean lie a number of treasures as well as poisons and dangers. We have to learn to recognize what is precious, and finally find Amrita – the secret of immortality or true happiness. The conflict is between our attachment to materialistic achievements, which gives us momentary happiness, but is a fantasy with no real basis (the domain of Rahu), and liberation of the soul, finding bliss and tranquillity, which is eternal and everlasting (Ketu is the Moksha karaka, significator for spiritual realization). The gods needed the help of Vasuki and in the same way we need the knowledge and direction provided by the wise nodes.

RAHU

It is special to Vedic astrology. It rules no Sun sign. Rahu rules the nakshatras Ardra, Swati and Shatabhishak
Rahu is the head part of the celestial snake. Lord Shiva has a snake around his neck; Lord Vishnu's throne was Shesh Naga – the eternal serpent. Shesh Naga represents the cycles of time and space, which seed the cosmic creation. The Nagas are shaped like snakes, but stand upright; they are highly evolved beings. They are wise, but their wisdom can be used for both good and bad. The Naga shedding his skin symbolizes transformation and rebirth. The snakes in Vedic literature serve to remind people of their mortality.

Rahu tempts people off their dharmic or correct path and onto the road of self-destruction. But Rahu has a very definite purpose for doing so. It wants you to learn, to taste and feel everything, so that from the full satiation of your senses you turn to the path of self-realization and find true enlightenment. Rahu, on a physical plane, gives you insatiable desire to achieve, to conquer. Once you have reached the pinnacle of achievement, you realize this success has not brought you happiness, because you were in fact chasing an illusion.

KETU

It is special to Vedic astrology. It rules no Sun sign. Ketu rules the nakshatras Ashwini, Magha and Mula
Ketu is the lower part of the celestial snake. Ketu has a variegated colour and therefore has the capacity to shine a light on you suddenly, bringing about enlightenment.

Ketu is born to the Jaimini family who followed the Mimasa School of philosophy. Their main concern was the correct interpretations of the Vedic rituals and settling any controversies about the Vedic texts. Ketu himself leads us, through meditation and intuitiveness, to true understanding of the universe, and guides the soul towards its final salvation.

Ketu is the planet of past life. It sets up many impediments, roadblocks and boulders in your journey through life. As you learn to understand karma you gradually start to let go of your karmic past and develop into a new person. It can be painful as you learn to let go of your material attachments. Ketu leads us towards eternal happiness, directing us towards moksha – the final liberation from the cycle of life and death.

Finding Your Sign

HOW TO DISCOVER NAKSHATRAS

For every one Western sign of the zodiac, there are three or four equivalent Indian signs, or nakshatras. Look up your Western sun sign in the left-hand column of the chart and read across to discover the corresponding nakshatra. The nakshatra wheel (following) shows the symbol for your nakshatra. Next, see pages 20–127 for a detailed character interpretation.

	WESTERN SUN SIGN	VEDIC NAKSHATRAS	
1	Aries 21 March to 20 April	Uttara Bhadra Revati Ashwini	21 to 31 March 31 March to 13 April 13 to 20 April
2	Taurus 21 April to 21 May	Ashwini Bharani Krittika	21 to 27 April 27 April to 11 May 11 to 21 May
3	Gemini 22 May to 21 June	Krittika Rohini Mrigasira Ardra	22 to 25 May 25 May to 8 June 8 to 21 June 21 June
4	Cancer 22 June to 23 July	Ardra Punarvasu Pushya	22 June to 5 July 5 to 19 July 19 to 23 July
5	Leo 24 July to 23 August	Pushya Ashlesha Magha	24 July to 2 August 2 to 16 August 16 to 23 August
6	Virgo 24 August to 23 September	Magha Purva Phalguni Uttara Phalguni	24 to 30 August 30 August to 13 September 13 to 23 September
7	Libra 24 September to 23 October	Uttara Phalguni Hasta Chitra Swati	24 to 26 September 26 September to 10 October 10 to 23 October 23 October
8	Scorpio 24 October to 22 November	Swati Vishakha Anuradha	24 October to 6 November 6 to 19 November 19 to 22 November
9	Sagittarius 23 November to 21 December	Anuradha Jyeshta Mula	23 November to 2 December 2 to 15 December 15 to 21 December
10	Capricorn 22 December to 20 January	Mula Purva Ashadha Uttara Ashadha	22 to 28 December 28 December to 11 January 11 to 20 January
11	Aquarius 21 January to 19 February	Uttara Ashadha Shravana Dhanishta Shatabhishak	21 to 24 January 24 January to 6 February 6 to 19 February 19 February
12	Pisces 20 February to 20 March	Shatabhishak Purva Bhadra Uttara Bhadra	20 February to 4 March 4 to 17 March 17 to 20 March

The symbols (known as glyphs) in the central segments of the wheel represent Western signs of the zodiac, whereas those on the outer ring of the wheel show the Nakshatra symbols. The symbols of the Nakshatras were chosen by *rishis*, or sages, and were meant both to reveal and conceal our subtle relationship with the heavens. For example, Shatabhishak, the twenty-fourth Nakshatra, is symbolized by stars, which denote an expansive outlook, but also represent the seventh chakra, one of the energy points of the body often used in acupuncture, yoga and reiki healing, indicating an understanding of the spirit through the earth.

MULA
JYESHTA
PURVA ASHADHA
ANURADHA
UTTARA ASHADHA
VISHAKHA
SHRAVANA
SAGITTARIUS
CAPRICORN
SCORPIO
SWATI
DHANISHTA
CHITRA
AQUARIUS
HASTA
SHATA-BHISHAK
LIBRA
PISCES
UTTARA PHALGUNI
PURVA BHADRA
VIRGO
PURVA PHALGUNI
UTTARA BHADRA
MAGHA
ARIES
REVATI
LEO
ASHWINI
ASHLESHA
TAURUS
CANCER
PUSHYA
BHARANI
GEMINI
KRITTIKA
ROHINI
MRIGASIRA
ARDRA
PUNARVASU

The Nakshatra Wheel

The Nakshatra Wheel represents a system of astrology that has been practised in India for over 5,000 years. The wheel is simple to use – you will find your sign in an instant – yet the knowledge will lead you along an ancient path of self-discovery.

Vedic astrology allocates three or four nakshatras to each sign of the zodiac. The nakshatras are connected to ancient myths, gods and symbols, and each has a particular animal sign. Knowledge about your nakshatra will give you in-depth information on character traits, emotional and spiritual patterns, as well as lucky colours, vowel sounds and names.

Ashwini

13 APRIL TO 27 APRIL

Key Words: Luminous and bright

Ruled by: Ketu	
Symbol: The horse's head	
Animal sign: Horse	
Deity: The Ashwini Kumaras	
Motivation: Dharma	
Guna triplicity: Rajas, Rajas, and Rajas	
Ayurvedic dosha: Vata	
Colour: Blood red	
Best direction: South	
Special consonants for birth names: Choo, Che, Cho, La	
Principal stars: Castor and Pollux	
Western signs: Aries (13 to 20 April) and Taurus (21 to 27 April)	

Symbol

ASHWA, THE HEAD OF THE HORSE

 The symbol of Ashwini is the horse, known in Sanskrit as 'Ashwa'. Ashwa is connected with the number seven. Seven is an auspicious number in Hindu philosophy. There are seven chakras – the creative energy which moves from the absolute within us – and seven flames of eternal fire – the seven states of wisdom. The horse is also a symbol of energy and vigour. These different creative energies need to be harnessed to achieve success.

Meaning and Mythology

Ashwini is named after the Ashwins, the twin sons of the Sun god. The Sun is meant to represent the parent – the root, the absolute. The divine link of the Sun to the first nakshatra means that an important evolutionary process is taking place with the help of the Sun, which gives energy to the whole process. Ashwins are the harbingers of usha or dawn. They are the link between the darkness of the night and the brightness of the dawn. Dawn brings with it the special energy of a new tomorrow, while still being attached to the mysterious past.

Ashwini, the first nakshatra, is ruled by Ketu and is partly in Aries and partly in Taurus. Aries deals with birth, new life, a freshness of approach and the start of a new cycle of life. Taurus nurtures our birth potential and allows us to develop our own personalities. Ashwini indicates the beginning of the soul's journey into the earthly life. Ketu is a mystical planet whose rulership of this part of the zodiac is full of occult significations. Ketu is the significator for moksha, the spiritual liberation, which allows our individual selves to merge with the divine consciousness. The beginning of the Indian zodiac by Ketu nakshatra shows that the true reason of our manifestation on earth is to find moksha. This is the stage where the mind is pure and we have not yet entangled ourselves into knots, which represent the attachments to life.

Ashwini has the nature of Shiva – the active energy represented by Aries – and Shakti – the passive female energy represented by Taurus. So there is a merging of male and female principles at the start of the zodiac.

Ruling deities

The ruling deities of Ashwini are the Ashwini Kumaras, the twin sons of the Sun god. The Ashwini Kumaras are physicians to the gods. They are beneficent and have great curative powers. They have the ability to restore youthfulness and rejuvenate the old. They are luminous in nature. They represent the duality to life – they are the connection between heaven and earth, day and night, past and future.

ASHWINI AIM IS FOR DHARMA

Ashwini expresses itself as dharmic. Dharma is the ethical use of religion, law, duty, and customs. Ashwini are concerned about leading a moral life. They have a strong sense of destiny and try to uphold the ethics of their country and religion. They can have a tendency to be self-righteous.

GUNA TRIPLICITY: RAJAS GUNA ON ALL LEVELS

The psychological quality of Ashwini is expressed in the guna of Rajas on all three levels of consciousness. Rajas indicates an outward search for the answers of life. The action principle dominates here. Rajasic people are driven by a great inner thirst; they are easily moved by their feelings. They are very active, mentally and physically, and are continually searching for new challenges. They are high achievers, and seek recognition, respect and success.

AYURVEDIC DOSHA IS VATA

Ashwini reflects the natural qualities of vata: action, sensation, perception, inspiration, communication and enthusiasm. Vata people tend to be of a nervous disposition. They are extremely active with lots of energy to expend. They have short attention spans and generally live on their nerves. They have to watch out for stress.

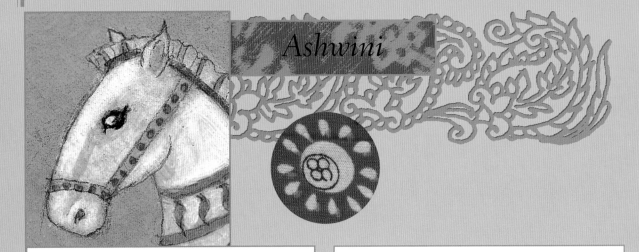

Ashwini

CHARACTERISTICS/ PERSONALITY TRAITS

Ashwini are the beautiful people of the zodiac. There is a special glow around them, which makes them extremely attractive to the opposite sex. They are strong, powerful and action-orientated. They always need new challenges and adventures in their lives. Nothing can be more debilitating for them than not having fresh goals to pursue; newness in life is their prime motivator. Although Ashwini express themselves chiefly through physical action, they also have a divine link to the hidden knowledge of life. They have a deeply intuitive nature, especially if they allow this to develop.

They are luminous, bright, beautiful and swift. They have open personalities, but there is a mysterious depth to them, which makes them hard to understand. Their representation of dawn indicates the link of their soul to the past. Ashwini are extremely idealistic. Their search for adventure and new experiences is linked to a pure and perfect view of the world, which they are seeking.

Ashwini are the natural healers of the zodiac and can be found in professions such as doctors, healers, and spiritualists. They can easily be misunderstood, as others do not always recognize their innocence and idealism.

HOW IT LINKS WITH THE WESTERN SUN SIGN AND RULER

Ashwini in Aries: Mars rules their outer energy and Ketu the inner self. Ketu is considered a spiritual warrior and Mars a physical one. This is useful in day-to-day life which they treat as a campaign, and they can be good planners and strategists. They find it difficult to accept failure.

Ashwini in Taurus: Venus rules their outer energy and Ketu the inner self. Venus is the only planet that knows the mantra of giving life to the dead. The link to healing is again very strong. Venus and Ketu combination indicates inner spirituality, but the outer self is slowly breaking away from its pure self and expressing life on a more worldly level.

SPIRITUAL LIFE PATH

Ashwini are linked to past lives and the soul's journey through its many manifestations. They will be deeply spiritual, but will not necessarily express it. They have a strong sense of duty in their lives, and they will be totally committed to their ultimate goals in life. They are beginning a new cycle of life lessons, and their spirituality has to be expressed by their actions in this life.

RELATIONSHIPS

They are looking for a partner who understands their need for freedom. They are idealistic in their relationships and are seeking someone who lives up to their high standards. Their ideal partner will be sporty, adventurous and active, with a deep inner spirituality. This is the dilemma facing Ashwini. They are seeking the perfect partner yet they are unable to commit.

SEXUAL ENERGY LINKED TO THE MALE HORSE

They are fiercely independent and beautiful. They need to roam free in wild pastures and it is not easy to tame them. Even the most domesticated Ashwini will always feel the call of the wild within them.

Male energy is the active principle. They need to conquer, and will not wait passively to express their desires. If they are attracted to someone, they will be the hunters. They are very sensuous, can be wonderful lovers and may even have a reputation as a sexual warrior. Sexual independence is the key word and commitment can be difficult for them.

FAMOUS ASHWINI

Peter Ustinov, Lucrezia Borgia, Queen Elizabeth II of England, Yehudi Menuhin, Leonardo da Vinci.

HOW ASHWINI RELATES TO OTHER NAKSHATRAS

Most compatible: The best partner for Ashwini is Bharani. Other fulfilling relationships for Ashwini will be with other Ashwini, Pushya, Ashlesha, Swati, Shravana and Revati. With Swati there will be few sexual sparks, so this partnership will have to work extra hard to keep passion alive.

Least compatible: Hasta, Uttara Phalguni, Jyeshta and Mula prove the most challenging for Ashwini. Hasta is too possessive for independent Ashwini. Hasta's ruler, the Moon, also has a very difficult relationship with Ketu, Ashwini's ruler. Uttara Phalguni obstructs Ashwini's personal growth; there is little support to keep this relationship special. Ashwini and Jyeshta have the ability to work through their differences, as Jyeshta's ruler, Mercury, is a friend of Ketu, and in the nakshatra support system, Jyeshta gives strength to Ashwini. Ketu also rules Mula. Ashwini and Mula cannot connect to each other because of their difficult karmic path, each having a different spiritual direction to take.

Ideal sexual partner: Ashwini, the male horse, connects passionately with the female horse, Shatabhishak. However, this relationship may not work in other areas. Ashwinis looking for a more complete relationship may not find satisfaction with this nakshatra.

Unsuitable sexual partners: Swati and Hasta are antagonistic to Ashwini. Their sexuality is linked to the buffalo, and as Ashwinis are fussy about their sexual partners, they may find these nakshatras too practical and sexually unimaginative. *For complete relationships information see pages 128–139.*

CUSPS

Those born at the end or beginning of the Ashwini should check the cusp details on page 140.

Bharani

27 APRIL TO 11 MAY

Key Word: Sensuality

Ruled by: Venus	
Symbol: Yoni, the female sexual organ	
Animal sign: Elephant	
Deity: Yama, the god of death	
Motivation: Artha	
Guna triplicity: Rajas, Rajas and Tamas	
Ayurvedic dosha: Pitta	
Colour: Blood red	
Best direction: West	
Special consonants for birth names: Li, Lu, Ley, Lo	
Principal stars: Al-Bhutain	
Western signs: Taurus	

Meaning and Mythology

Bharani is wholly in the sign of Taurus. Venus rules both signs. The strong Venusian influence gives this nakshatra an intense attraction, a love of luxuries and the desire for sexual expression. 'Bharani' means 'cherishing', 'supporting' and 'nourishing'. Bharani expresses feminine energy in its pure form.

Its basic principle is Shakti – the passive female power. Female energy has an important place in Vedic philosophy. It is this energy that incubates the soul and transports it from one realm of existence to another.

Bharani rules beauty, femininity, elegance and the aspiration for the good things of life. People born under Bharani are usually beautiful. Their attraction is earthy and sensuous. It is not easy for everyone to understand the attraction of Bharani people, but they will never lack attention from the opposite sex. They usually have a curious mixture of quiet charm combined with strong sexuality radiating from within.

Bharani people sometimes do things to excess. Whether they are indulging in sex or practising yoga, they often do not know when to stop. They are idealists and want others to live up to their high expectations. There is a darker side to their nature, which is symbolized by the god Yama, who rules darkness. Although they are idealists, they also have a mystifying depth that attracts male energy to the passive but extremely electrifying force of Bharani.

Symbol

YONI, THE FEMALE SEXUAL ORGAN

The symbol for Bharani is Yoni, the female reproductive organ. This establishes Bharani as a channel for creation whether by the sexual act or by other creative energies. In India, certain ancient monuments, such as Khajurao, celebrate the female sexuality in their immense sculptures. The female sexual organ is very important if the soul has to be transported from one life to another. Bharani acts as the channel for taking the soul from a spiritual manifestation to a more material one.

Ruling deities

The presiding deities of Ashlesha are the Nagas. Nagas are snakes who have great occult powers. The snake carries his poison in a pouch. but will only use this when forced to do so. As the poison can be used for healing or for killing, so the Nagas have the capacity for both good and bad. Ashlesha can lead people to knowledge and wisdom, but it can also take them down the path of danger.

ASHLESHA AIM IS FOR DHARMA

Ashlesha is connected to achieving its destiny and dharma plays an important part of acting out their given karma. Ashlesha will always try to do the right thing. They understand the importance of their spiritual responsibilities and expressing them through the right actions.

GUNA TRIPLICITY: RAJAS, SATTVA AND SATTVA

The psychological quality of Punarvasu is expressed in the guna of Rajas on the primary (physical) level, Sattva on the secondary (mental) level and on the tertiary (spiritual) level. Ashlesha are restless and forever seeking answers. But the Sattva of their inner self gives them a deep calmness and spirituality. Whatever conflicts Ashlesha face, they have the ability of acceptance and inner spiritual purity that guides them towards their goals. Ashlesha will always seek to express their inner self.

AYURVEDIC DOSHA IS KAPHA

Ashlesha have philosophical, calm and patient natures. They are emotional and sentimental. They are able to retain knowledge and are practical in outlook. Under Ashlesha, they can learn to be calm in mind, although, at times, this can lead to mental inertia.

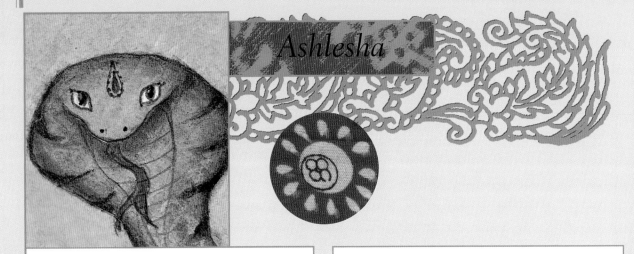

Ashlesha

CHARACTERISTICS/ PERSONALITY TRAITS

Ashlesha usually have hypnotic eyes and the power to tantalize. They have the ability to look deep within people and have incisive vision that enables them to look into the hidden secrets of nature and understand true wisdom. They do not believe in wasting energy and may appear lazy, but this is deceptive – their minds are always active.

Ashlesha often live alone or are loners. They are independent, and not very keen to have children. Their creativity is linked to ideas. They appreciate calmness and tranquillity, and enjoy meditating. They would be natural for yoga: they are supple and aim for the highest spiritual aspirations.

Ashlesha are witty with a sharp humour. The wisdom they carry from their past lives makes them intelligent and wise advisers. They also understand destiny, so they will not fight against restrictions imposed by their past karma.

They are usually very attractive and are not above using their looks to get what they want. Ashlesha love beautiful clothes, although they seldom dress in an ostentatious manner. They are softly spoken, hardly ever raising their voices, but others will listen to them. It takes a lot to make them angry, but if aroused, it is best to stay well clear of them.

Ashlesha are ambitious and successful and make good politicians. They may decide on a complete change of career several times in life. With their many talents, they can go from being doctors to actors or vice versa.

On the negative side, Ashlesha can be vindictive, sarcastic and vicious.

HOW IT LINKS WITH THE WESTERN SUN SIGN AND RULER

Ashlesha in Leo: Ashlesha expresses the Sun/Mercury combination. It is one of intellect and power. These people are bright, clever and sharp. Mercury deals with knowledge in duality. The Sun is steady, and it offers Ashlesha stability for the intellectual search to operate. Ashlesha are not afraid to show their talents in public.

SPIRITUAL LIFE PATH

Ashlesha's spiritual path is to recognize their destiny. They need to accept that they are responsible for what they experience. Ashlesha will always try to do what they feel is right. Ashlesha are at the end of one cycle and are beginning another. They need to become prepared to express their knowledge through work in this lifetime. Their spiritual path is connected to the material world.

Ruling deities

The ruling deity is Yama. Yama can be interpreted in two forms. The first is as the god of death. Death does not necessarily mean physical death, it can also mean the ending of one chapter of your life, and moving on to another with fresh energy. The other meaning of Yama is connected with yoga. In yoga, Yama (restraint) and Niyama (practice or observation) are used to channel physical energies.

BHARANI AIM IS FOR ARTHA

Bharani is motivated by artha, which is activity on a material plane. People born in Bharani are largely materialistic unless they voluntarily decide to harness their inner spirituality by some means; for example, by practising yoga. The rulership of Venus makes the action very much on a material plane.

GUNA TRIPLICITY: RAJAS, RAJAS AND TAMAS

The psychological quality of Bharani is expressed in the guna of Rajas on the primary (physical) level and secondary (mental) level. On the tertiary (spiritual) level, the guna is Tamas, which adds a kind of darkness or a subtle knot in their personalities. Rajas indicates an outward search for answers. Tamasic people have a mental attitude that emphasizes sensuality. The Rajas/Tamas psychological combination brings forth a mysterious quality, and a restless idealism with intense sexuality.

AYURVEDIC DOSHA IS PITTA

Bharani reflects the dosha of pitta or the fiery quality. Bharani are active, motivated and hot-tempered. They tend to be creative, knowledgeable and intelligent. Bharani are full of heat and passion, but they have a tendency to burn out quickly. They need to calm their temperament with cool colours, food and places.

Bharani

CHARACTERISTICS/ PERSONALITY TRAITS

Bharani are the sensualists of the zodiac. They are forever searching for their spiritual self, but are usually happiest when expressing their sensual nature. Bharani should accept their sensuality, and allow their sexual energy to become a creative channel. If they do not learn how to focus their energies, they can have a tendency to get overly concerned with sex and may become promiscuous.

Bharani enjoy the good things in life. They admire all forms of beauty and arts. They are sometimes aggressive and can appear selfish. Bharani can be goal-orientated, and always on the move.

They love jewellery and good food. If you want to woo a Bharani person, buy them an exquisite perfume – their sense of smell is acute and very refined. They like the real thing. Bharani love to touch and cuddle; they have a need for physical closeness.

Bharani are constantly trying to harmonize their inner needs with their outer self, but this is almost impossible since the two are in conflict. It would benefit them to practise yoga, as this is the nakshatra most closely connected with yoga. Bharani also need to practise temperance and patience. They can overdo things.

They are highly individualistic, and often have larger than life personalities. With their love of good food and wine, they tend to put on weight. They are extremely strong and are not afraid of hard work. They can just as easily do hard manual labour as perform delicate tasks with great precision.

HOW IT LINKS WITH THE WESTERN SUN SIGN AND RULER

Bharani in Taurus: Venus rules both outer energy and the inner self. Bharani adopts the qualities of Venus: diplomacy, creativity, great charm, and a love for beauty, music, art and relationships. Bharani symbolizes fertility, harmony and growth. These people see their sexuality as an expression of divinity.

SPIRITUAL LIFE PATH

Bharani's spiritual life is connected to the journey from the abstract to the real. They are still connected to the subtle energies, but are aware that the true expression of their spirituality has to be in the physical and material world. They express it through creating and nurturing new life, and by allowing the soul to express itself in the material realm. Because of their outwardly sexual and practical natures their spiritual side is often misunderstood.

RELATIONSHIPS

These earthy people need a partner who can give them long-term commitment. For a relationship to succeed, they need partners who can match their earthiness and sensuality. They will fight for and relentlessly pursue the person who takes their fancy. They enjoy the thrill of the chase and the final victory! However, once they have won the partner of their choice, they can become bored easily or start to take their partners for granted.

SEXUAL ENERGY LINKED TO THE MALE ELEPHANT

They like their independence, only seeking out partners when they are ready. They enjoy competition and will do anything to win sexual favours from a lover. But Bharani do not always devote the same amount of attention to their partners after mating. They may not have lost interest in them, but there are other practical tasks to be completed before they can resume their intense passion. They can be aggressive and possessive, and like to be in control. This applies equally to men and women.

FAMOUS BHARANI

William Hurst, Rudolph Valentino, Tony Blair, Saddam Hussein, Eva Perón, Karl Marx.

HOW BHARANI RELATES TO OTHER NAKSHATRAS

Most compatible: Ashwini is the best partner for Bharani. Other relationships that Bharani will find satisfying are with other Bharani, Punarvasu, Swati, Uttara Ashadha and Shravana.

Least compatible: Uttara Bhadra is the most difficult relationship for Bharani. Uttara Bhadra is a spiritually inclined nakshatra while Bharani want to experience sensuality and material happiness. This can create coldness and lack of empathy, and can lead to unhappiness. Chitra and Bharani are both strong sexually. Their planetary rulers, Mars and Venus, indicate passion, but it is the sort of passion that can die out quickly, leaving little behind to tie them together. Dhanishta is a poor sexual partner for Bharani, and for Bharani to consider a relationship without sex would be to go against their nature, and would simply create frustration and loneliness.

Ideal sexual partner: Bharani, the male elephant, connects intimately with the female elephant, Revati. Both enjoy sex. As Revati and Bharani are also compatible in other areas, this can be a relationship that brings immense happiness.

Unsuitable sexual partners: Dhanishta and Purva Bhadra are sexually incompatible with Bharani. The elephant and the lion are adversaries in the wilderness and this creates incompatibility in their sexual needs. Sex is important to Bharani and they should try to avoid sexually challenging relationships with these nakshatras. *For complete relationships information see pages 128–139.*

CUSPS

Those born at the end or beginning of the Bharani should check the cusp details on page 140.

Krittika

11 MAY TO 25 MAY

Key Words: Fire, warmth and power

Ruled by: The Sun	
Symbol: Razor	
Animal sign: Sheep	
Deity: Agni, the god of fire	
Motivation: Kama	
Guna triplicity: Rajas, Rajas and Sattva	
Ayurvedic dosha: Kapha	
Colour: White	
Best direction: North	
Special consonants for birth names: Aa, I, U, Ae	
Principal stars: Alcyone	
Western signs: Taurus (11 to 21 May) and Gemini (22 to 25 May)	

Symbol
RAZOR

The symbol for Krittika is the razor. The razor or knife can be used both constructively and destructively. This symbol highlights the main aspect of Krittika: the negative and positive forces within them. In the same way that a doctor uses a razor to cut through infected organs, Krittika can be relentless in cutting out negativity from their lives.

Meaning and Mythology

Krittika is mostly in the western sign of Taurus and its final part is in Gemini. Venus rules Taurus, Mercury rules Gemini, and the Sun rules Krittika. Solar energy is very strong in Krittika, with outer influences by Venus and Mercury.

Krittika consists of six visible stars and one invisible star. This is the constellation Pleiades. They are considered wives of the seven great rishis, great teachers who astronomically make up the stars of Ursa Major. The Vedas say that the seventh invisible star is married to Dhruva – the pole star. The relationship of Krittika and the pole star emphasizes its role in the importance of invisible laws of nature.

The myth of Krittika is connected to the demon Taraka and the birth of Kartika, the warrior Mars. Taraka had got the blessing of Brahma, the creator of the universe, that only a seven-day-old son of Shiva could kill him. Shiva had no intention of producing a son. So Kamadeva, the god of love, shot an arrow towards Shiva as he meditated in the Himalayas. By this means, the gods obtained his semen and Krittikas incubated it. From that seed, Kartika, the warrior god, was born. He destroyed Taraka when he was seven days old.

Krittika is passive. It has both constructive and destructive principles. Like a mother, Krittika does not know how her progeny will turn out. It places the responsibility of how to live life firmly on the individual. Krittika people can become healers or warriors. They will have immense courage and confidence. Krittika has the capacity to create powerful people who are not afraid to confront difficult situations. The ability to control the mind is strong here.

Ruling deities

Agni, the sacred fire, represents the fire of the mind, the flames of aspiration and the blaze of intellect. Agni represents the seven flames that allow the seven levels of consciousness to operate. In India it forms the centre of the marriage ceremony. Couples tie their lives together in physical and spiritual knots with Agni as their witness. Agni is also the Kundalini, our latent fire, in the spine.

KRITTIKA AIM IS FOR KAMA

Kama motivates Krittika. Kama is desires and needs on a practical level. Krittika people are full of passion and have the courage to fulfil very difficult responsibilities. Krittika is a very virile nakshatra and therefore they are also likely to be passionate about sexual relationships.

THE GUNA TRIPLICITY: RAJAS, RAJAS AND SATTVA

Rajas on a physical and mental level indicate an outward search for the answers of life. Sattva is calmness and peace. Their outer persona is that of a warrior, but the sattva psychology in their personality reflects calmness. They will only fight so that peace can reign. The Rajas/Sattva combination is difficult to understand. Wherever Krittikas go, there is sure to be a storm. However, when you get close to these people you will understand their inner quietness and search for peace.

AYURVEDIC DOSHA IS KAPHA

The Krittika dosha is kapha. They are philosophical, calm, and have patient natures. Krittika's ability to remain calm in the face of great adversity makes them exceptional commanders and leaders. However, laziness and weight management can be a problem.

Krittika

CHARACTERISTICS/ PERSONALITY TRAITS

Krittika are the puritans of the zodiac. They are dedicated and extremely intelligent. They are natural warriors, with an instinct to defend and protect. Krittika people can stay cool and collected in a crisis. However, they can anger easily. They do not necessarily like confrontations, but they will not shy away from difficult situations.

Krittika people often have a showbiz type persona. They may have two sides to their personality: an outgoing extrovert and a puritan. You will find both priests and entertainers among the Krittika. The singer Cher is a perfect example of the Krittika personality. She is larger than life; she is intelligent and talented; there appears to be a lack of commitment in her relationships.

Krittika have many admirers. They attract attention, not only because of their striking looks, but also because of their intelligence and brightness.

Krittika know that the fire burning within them can be destructive, if allowed to rage uncontrolled. They should learn early on how to harness it. This sign has strong links to yoga, the science of self-discipline, which Krittika have plenty of.

HOW IT LINKS WITH THE WESTERN SUN SIGN AND RULER

Krittika in Taurus: Venus rules the outer energy and the Sun Krittika's inner self. This gives outer sensuality with inner purity. Taurus is a sign of hard work; under Krittika's influence these people will achieve power and influence in the world. Krittika/Taurus thus reflects the harnessing of creative power.

Krittika in Gemini: Outer energy is ruled by Mercury, and the inner is ruled by the Sun. This shows a great emphasis on intellect; they will use their minds to try to improve the world they live in. Krittika/Gemini can have two distinct personalities.

SPIRITUAL LIFE PATH

The linking of Krittika to the Kundalini and yoga shows a person aware of their latent power, yet there is a part of them that they do not understand. Krittika have the ability to purify themselves and take their body through a 'trial by fire' to find their inner core. Krittika people are always searching for their invisible self. They need to understand their inner fire in order to find spiritual peace, and they can be great thinkers.

RELATIONSHIPS

Krittika are passionate and sensuous, but they may be afraid to take the final step towards commitment. They will always keep a part of themselves hidden. They like to cuddle and be part of the relationship. Krittika are fighters, but they will not fight for relationships. They will walk away if they have to fight for a partner. However, if you offer Krittika unconditional love, they will be there for you.

SEXUAL ENERGY LINKED TO THE FEMALE SHEEP

Sheep like to be part of the herd. They are skittish and playful. They will flee from, rather than fight for their mate. The female sexuality shows a passive side of Krittika. Both male and female Krittika like to be chased and will not show interest unless they know a partner is interested. They may be leaders in every other aspect of life, but when it comes to expressing their sexuality they become passive spectators. Krittika are late developers as far as their sexuality is concerned.

FAMOUS KRITTIKA

Stevie Wonder, Harold Robbins, Laurence Olivier, George Lucas, Cher, Jim Jones.

HOW KRITTIKA RELATES TO OTHER NAKSHATRAS

Most compatible: Jyeshta is the best partner for Krittika. Jyeshta want love, and Krittika can give them strength and security. Krittika will enjoy Jyeshta's possessiveness. Other relationships that work well for Krittika are Pushya and Shatabhishak.

Least compatible: One of the notable features of Krittika is that it does not have totally negative compatibility with any other nakshatra. Rohini, Swati, Uttara Ashadha and Revati are the nakshatras that prove the most difficult for Krittika. Rohini will be too emotional for Krittika, while they find it hard to trust Swati completely. Uttara Ashadha is a loner and so is Krittika. They are both ruled by fire; this is what will attract them as well as split them apart. Revati are mystical, and are not interested in power – the domain of Krittika. They can never appreciate Krittika's good qualities.

Ideal sexual partner: Krittika, the female sheep, enjoys a passionate relationship with the male sheep, Pushya. Pushya bring out the best in Krittika. They are also compatible in most other areas of life and their sexual compatibility adds extra pizzazz.

Unsuitable sexual partners: Monkeys, Purva Ashadha and Shravana, are sexually incompatible with the placid sheep, Krittika. Monkeys are naughty, manipulative and complicated, and they can often be too devious for the straightforward sheep. Monkeys cannot give Krittika the sexual loyalty that they need.

For complete relationships information see pages 128–139.

CUSPS

Those born at the end or beginning of the Krittika should check the cusp details on page 140.

Rohini

25 May to 8 June

Key Words: Beauty and passion

Ruled by: The Moon	
Symbol: Chariot	
Animal sign: Serpent	
Deity: Brahma, the creator	
Motivation: Moksha	
Guna triplicity: Rajas, Tamas and Rajas	
Ayurvedic dosha: Kapha	
Colour: White	
Best direction: East	
Special consonants for birth names: Au, Va, Vi, Vo	
Principal stars: Aldebaran	
Western signs: Gemini	

Symbol
Chariot

The symbol is the chariot. Chariots are traditionally seen as luxury transport, used by royalty. This links all kinds of comforts and luxuries to Rohini. Rohini like to live in style and enjoy the sensual side of nature. On a spiritual level, the chariot transports the soul to the material realm in comfort, and protects it while it prepares to face its earthly responsibilities.

Meaning and Mythology

In Sanskrit 'Rohini' means 'red', which suggests passion and sensuality. Rohini is in the sign of Gemini, ruled by Mercury. Rohini is essentially about mental pursuits. In Indian astrology, both the Moon and Mercury reflect the mind: the Moon represents the complete mind and Mercury the rational part of it.

The essence of Rohini is that they appear detached and unemotional on the outside – characteristics of Mercury – but their inner core is full of emotions, romanticism and love.

Rohini is considered to be the favourite wife of the Moon. (According to the mythology the 27 nakshatras are the 27 wives of the Moon, with whom he stayed for one day a month.) The other wives, jealous of the Moon's infatuation with Rohini, complained to Brahma, the creator, who cursed the Moon to lose all his power, but then let him regain it. This is reflected in the Moon's waxing and waning cycles.

The Moon's infatuation with Rohini reflects the soul's entanglement with the material world. It loses its purpose and becomes involved with the earthly illusions, which directly leads to the loss of purity. Rohini heralds the waxing and waning of life, the ever-constant cycles of life and death. Rohini involves people in sensuous pleasures; it heightens the attachment to earthly desires. It directs the soul towards the physical world with its pleasures and pains.

Ruling deities

The ruling deity is Brahma, the creator of the universe and one of the main Vedic gods. Brahma represents infinity; all individuals are supposed to be part of Brahma and connected to the universal soul. Rohini's link with Brahma indicates a desire to merge with the absolute. Rohini expresses this through its desire for relationships, needing divine love to feel complete.

ROHINI AIM IS FOR MOKSHA

Rohini's motivation is moksha, which means finding spiritual realization. However, at this stage, that realization must come from intense involvement in earthly passion. There is an underlying sense of mission. Rohini find enlightenment through devotion – to a lover, spouse or god. This can lead to Rohini people feeling incomplete within themselves.

GUNA TRIPLICITY: RAJAS, TAMAS AND RAJAS

The psychological quality of Rohini is expressed in the guna of Rajas on the primary (physical) level, Tamas on the secondary (mental) level and Rajas on the tertiary (spiritual) level. Outwardly there appears to be a search for answers, but the mental self can sometimes be too lazy and involved in the material world of desires. The subtle connection to Rajas indicates their never-ending search for an ideal. Rohini are always searching for the perfect partner. Their discontentment can lead them to break up good relationships in the search for a better partner.

AYURVEDIC DOSHA IS KAPHA

The Rohini dosha is kapha. Kapha signifies the water quality. Water is necessary for sustenance. These people are emotional and sentimental. Rohini can become too entangled in their emotions and this can create difficulties for them. They may also have problems with their weight.

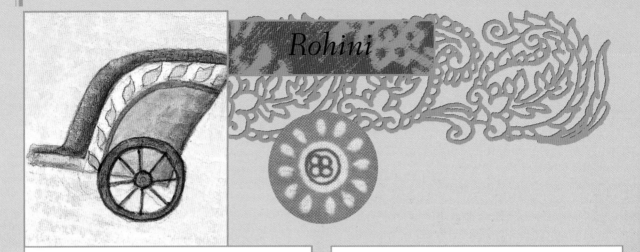

Rohini

CHARACTERISTICS/ PERSONALITY TRAITS

Rohini indicates great beauty, perfection, and a striving towards feminine essence. Both male and female Rohini are extremely attractive. Even the male Rohini have a feminine quality in their emotional natures and this gives them the ability to understand the feelings of others.

Rohini are sensitive and can be hurt easily. They are emotional, changeable, mysterious and charming. They have much love to give, and they need devotion in return.

Rohini people are possessive. They find it difficult to let go. They can become too inflamed by their passions, whether it is for a person or an ideology. Rohini should be careful around alcohol or other intoxicants, as they have a tendency to become addicted.

As Rohini is a sign that seeks moksha or enlightenment, they can sometimes undervalue themselves. They may suffer from poor self-image or get involved in complex relationships and triangles in love. On the negative side, they can be vindictive and extremely jealous.

Rohini's need for love and romance is supreme. They are true romantics at heart, willing to sacrifice almost anything for love. However, meeting them for the first time, you may find them detached. You need to truly understand Rohini to appreciate their romantic natures. Rohini want all the luxuries of life. They are not prepared to slum it, even for the sake of romance.

HOW IT LINKS WITH THE WESTERN SUN SIGN AND RULER

Rohini in Gemini: Mercury rules Gemini and the Moon rules this nakshatra. Therefore, Rohini are dominated by the mind. They will be analytical, yet romantic at the same time. They need to be stimulated intellectually as they get bored easily. They can be over-emotional. Creativity is their forte; Rohini creativity is linked to intellect, ideas and beauty. They can be moody and mysterious, making it hard for others to understand them.

SPIRITUAL LIFE PATH

Rohini spirituality is linked with the connection of their individual self to the absolute. As Rohini's role is in the material world, they need to express it through love and devotion. This devotion has to be so great that they break down any barriers between themselves and the object of their love. This love is pure and idealistic. They may make sacrifices in pursuit of their final goal of eternal happiness.

RELATIONSHIPS

Rohini want a mate for life. They need to love completely, wholeheartedly and unconditionally. They may present a different face to the world, but their inner self is always seeking love. Rohini have the ability to delude themselves. They may get involved with people who are not completely faithful, and they should be wary of their desire for the perfect relationship. They may be involved in a good relationship, yet feel dissatisfied. They may become deeply unhappy if they seek new relationships in the hope of finding perfection.

SEXUAL ENERGY LINKED TO THE MALE SERPENT

Potential mates find each other by sending out special 'scent messages'. The male snake will rub the female snake with his head as part of their courtship. They want a partner for life and generally find one. Rohini is the male snake. This suggests that Rohini will actively express their sexuality. They are not afraid to pursue the object of their affections and can be hypnotic in their attraction. Once Rohini have decided on their mate, they will plan their wooing meticulously. However, they do need to get subtle signals from a potential mate before they will take the first step.

FAMOUS ROHINI

Ian Fleming, Marilyn Monroe, Thomas Hardy, Clint Eastwood, Prince Rainier III of Monaco.

HOW ROHINI RELATES TO OTHER NAKSHATRAS

Most compatible: Rohini completely connects with Anuradha, the most compatible nakshatra. Anuradha are searching for idealistic love and Rohini are seeking passion. Together they have the capacity to fulfil each other. Mrigasira, Pushya, Anuradha, Shatabhishak, and Uttara Bhadra all satisfy Rohini's need for love in their different ways. Pushya love Rohini unconditionally, Shatabhishak ignites Rohini's inner passions, and Uttara Bhadra are a perfect foil for Rohini's exotic personality.

Least compatible: Rohini's lunar rulership allows them to relate to other nakshatras. Although Krittika, Magha, Ashlesha, and Vishakha teach Rohini the most difficult lessons in relationships, they are able to work on and nurture even the most complicated of relationships. Krittika cannot fulfil Rohini emotionally; Ashlesha are too involved in spiritual awakening to give unconditional love to Rohini, Magha can reject and hurt them and Vishakha are too restless for the possessive Rohini.

Ideal sexual partner: Mrigasira, the male snake, makes the best sexual partner for Rohini. They understand each other's sexual needs perfectly. They are also compatible in other areas of life, so this can be a mutually satisfying relationship all round.

Unsuitable sexual partners: The mongoose (Uttara Ashadha) is a deadly enemy to the snake in the wild and therefore Rohini should avoid a sexual relationship with this nakshatra.
For complete relationships information see pages 128–139.

CUSPS

Those born at the end or beginning of the Rohini should check the cusp details on page 140.

Mrigasira

8 JUNE TO 21 JUNE

Key Words: Intellectual warrior

Ruled by: Mars	
Symbol: Head of the deer	
Animal sign: Serpent	
Deity: Soma, the Moon god	
Motivation: Moksha	
Guna triplicity: Rajas, Tamas and Tamas	
Ayurvedic dosha: Pitta	
Colour: Silver	
Best direction: South	
Special consonants for birth names: Ke, Ko, Ha, Hi	
Principal stars: Orion	
Western signs: Gemini	

Symbol
HEAD OF THE DEER

The symbol for Mrigasira is the head of the deer. The deer is a symbol of the Moon. According to Indian mythology, the shadows on the lunar surface are supposed to represent the head of the deer. This makes birth in Mrigasira very auspicious. It gives these people a special sensitivity.

Mrigasira essentially shows the beginning of search in the world of illusions. The deer is the golden deer that we all search for, but can never find. This leads to dissatisfaction with their circumstances in life.

Meaning and Mythology

'Mriga' means 'a deer' and 'Sira' means 'head'. The head of the deer is also a symbol of the Moon. It is ruled by Mars – the planet of action and adventure. Mrigasira is situated in the sign of Gemini. Its outer energy is ruled by Mercury and the inner self by Mars. Mrigasira is considered the nakshatra where intellect is born. Mars, its ruler, allows us to be adventurous – giving immense courage, not only physically, but also to move into new areas intellectually.

To understand the impact of Mrigasira on the intellect, we need to look into the myth of Tara. In the Vedas, there is a story known as Tara's Rahasya (Tara's secret). Tara was the wife of Brihaspati (Jupiter), but she had an affair with Soma (the Moon) and eloped with him. Brihaspati wanted her back, but she refused. A great war ensued in the heavens. The gods sided with Brihaspati, and Venus and the demons sided with Soma. Finally, Brahma intervened and Tara returned to Brihaspati. Tara was already pregnant and the child from her affair with Soma was Buddha (Mercury).

Mrigasira indicates the birth of Buddhi or intellect. For intellect to be born there had to be a merging of the godly impulses of Tara with the earthly impulses of the Moon. The Moon represents the whole mind and Mercury, as the son of the Moon, is a fragment of the whole mind, the intellect. The godly and the earthly impulses of his parents represent the duality of Mercury.

Ruling deities

Mrigasira's ruling deity is Soma, which is another name for the Moon. Soma is also a mystical nectar that enhances the mind and its faculties. There is a passion for learning in this sign.

MRIGASIRA AIM IS FOR MOKSHA

Mrigasira motivation is moksha or reaching for spiritual realization, but at this stage that realization has to come from intense involvement in earthly passion. There is an underlying sense of mission. The involvement is with the earthly matters but the final destination is eternal happiness.

GUNA TRIPLICITY: RAJAS, TAMAS AND TAMAS

The psychological quality of Mrigasira is expressed in the guna of Rajas on the primary (physical), Tamas on the secondary (mental) level and Tamas on the tertiary (spiritual) level. Although outwardly there appears to be a search for answers, the inner self is involved in the material world of desires. There is a restlessness, which keeps them searching for answers throughout life. Their inner self is attracted to the material impulses.

AYURVEDIC DOSHA IS PITTA

Mrigasira reflects the dosha of pitta, the fiery quality. They are intelligent, perceptive and discriminating. They have a fiery intellect and are natural leaders, but they can anger very easily. Mrigasira people are active and motivated. They tend to be creative, knowledgeable and intelligent. They can burn out quickly.

Mrigasira

CHARACTERISTICS/ PERSONALITY TRAITS

Mrigasira are generally tall and slim, with large, expressive eyes. They have a strong individuality. They can be charismatic, sharply intelligent and witty. They take pleasure in pitting their intellect against others, and enjoy winning debates and arguments.

They are action-oriented and enjoy sports of all kinds. It is usually impossible for them to sit still for long as they need to face new challenges all the time.

On the negative side, they can be fickle. Their need for constant excitement means they can get bored easily. It will be difficult for them to commit to any one thing, as there are always new ideas, hobbies, jobs and relationships to entice them.

Mrigasira are strong-willed and impulsive. However, they may lack confidence in their own abilities. Their natural tendency is to be defensive and they are likely to be sensitive to criticism. They need to appreciate themselves.

They express their passions with great drama. As they are natural leaders, they need to be in positions of authority and power over others.

HOW IT LINKS WITH THE WESTERN SUN SIGN AND RULER

Mrigasira in Gemini: Mercury rules Gemini and Mars rules this nakshatra. The Mercury/Mars relationship is considered difficult. Mars is the planet of action and Mercury of intellect. This gives Mrigasira a sharp and aggressive intelligence. The Mars/Mercury combination gives a great talent for writing. Many writers and authors are born under this nakshatra. Mrigasira are considered to be intellectual warriors.

SPIRITUAL LIFE PATH

Mrigasira are at the beginning of the search from within. But to truly find themselves, they will need to look for answers in the outer world. They may feel dissatisfied with the present circumstances of their life. Their strong sense of individuality could hamper the search for their spiritual self.

RELATIONSHIPS

Mrigasira are looking for intellectually satisfying relationships. They need a partner who is their equal. They can be detached and aloof, so they may find it difficult to make a total commitment. When they find a partner who meets their high expectations, it can be a passionate relationship.

SEXUAL ENERGY LINKED TO THE FEMALE SERPENT

Potential mates find each other by sending out special 'scent messages'. The male snake will rub the female snake with his head as part of their courtship. They want a partner for life, and generally find one.

Mrigasira's mating rituals are similar to those of the serpents. Mrigasira is the female snake. Female here means for passive energy. Mrigasira will not be an aggressive partner. They may need someone else to take the first steps in a sexual relationship. The serpent sexuality is intensely private and passionate. These people can hypnotize others with their sensual powers. They will keep their sexuality under wraps, and only a person whom they truly desire can activate their inner passion.

HOW MRIGASIRA RELATES TO OTHER NAKSHATRAS

Most compatible: Hasta provides the best relationship for Mrigasira. Mrigasira relates to Hasta's emotional self, while Hasta fulfils Mrigasira's intellectual desires and needs.

Rohini, Ardra and Revati also connect well. Love thrives between Mrigasira and Rohini, and Ardra is a partner of intellectual equality. Revati love Mrigasira unconditionally and a deep connection is established.

Least compatible: Mrigasira do not have any nakshatra that is extremely negative for them. They have an instinctive ability to work with even the most complex people. However, Pushya, Chitra and Purva Ashadha are the nakshatras that they will have greatest difficulty with. Pushya can appear too rigid; this is a relationship that needs time to develop. As Chitra are dynamic and powerful, they are similar to Mrigasira, and this relationship can become too competitive. Purva Ashadha's capricious nature will drive Mrigasira mad – for this relationship to develop further, both partners will have to work really hard.

Ideal sexual partner: Rohini, the female snake, is the best sexual partner for Mrigasira. They have much common ground, which allows their relationship to flourish on many levels.

Unsuitable sexual partners: The Mongoose (Uttara Ashadha) is a deadly enemy to the snake in the wild and therefore Mrigasira should avoid a sexual relationship with this nakshatra. Mrigasira has the ability to connect to Uttara Ashadha in other areas of compatibility, but they should always remember the hidden undercurrents of sexual rivalry and anger, and their inimical natures.

For complete relationships information see pages 128–139.

CUSPS

Those born at the end or beginning of the Mrigasira should check the cusp details on page 140.

FAMOUS MRIGASIRA

Prince William, Cole Porter, Che Guevara, Paul McCartney, Jean-Paul Sartre.

Ardra

21 June to 5 July

Key Words: Political strategist

Ruled by: Rahu	
Symbol: The jewel or the head	
Animal sign: Dog	
Deity: Rudra, the god of destruction	
Motivation: Kama	
Guna triplicity: Rajas, Tamas and Sattva	
Ayurvedic dosha: Vata	
Colour: Green	
Best direction: West	
Special consonants/vowels: Koo, Kha, Ang, Chha	
Principal stars: Al-Han'ah	
Western signs: Gemini (21 June) and Cancer (21 June to 5 July)	

Symbol
Jewel or the Head

 The symbol of the jewel indicates the ability to absorb the kinetic, mystical and spiritual energies from the Sun. Jewels absorb the energies around them and transmit them to the wearer. Ardra have the capacity to absorb these powers and can use them for good or bad. The other symbol of Ardra is the head where the brain or the mind is situated. The brain is formed by experiences from past karma. How we react in this life is determined by the sum total of the experiences of these karmas.

Meaning and Mythology

'Ardra' means 'green, moist'. The first day of Ardra is situated in Gemini, ruled by Mercury, and the rest is situated in Cancer, which is ruled by the Moon. Rahu rules Ardra. This rulership of Rahu and the Moon and Mercury explains the field of operation for Ardra. Recall the story of Rahu, as the demon Vasuki (on page 16), who drank the nectar to make himself immortal, and you will understand why Ardra's ruler wants it to achieve the highest ambitions. The Moon/Mercury relationship indicates that Ardra's sphere of activity is connected to the mind, emotionally and intellectually. Rahu makes us want to achieve the impossible and reach for our highest aspirations; then makes us realize the futility of this. Achievement in itself does not bring satisfaction. The search is for intellectual perfection, but this can create dissatisfaction with life.

The overall influence of Ardra represents the intuitiveness and sensitivity of the Moon, the intellectual power of Mercury, and the lust for immortality represented by Rahu. The Rahu/Mercury combination makes for the pursuit of intellectual excellence. The Rahu/Moon combination is complicated. They have a karmic relationship that is linked to finding eternal happiness. Rahu has the ability to eclipse the Moon; this gives people born under Ardra an inner darkness that they are perpetually fighting against. Ardra can create problems for themselves; they may become self-destructive as they try to create an idealistic state of affairs.

Ardra want to achieve the impossible and if they fail to do this they can regard themselves as failures.

Ruling deities

Rudra, the god of destruction, is the presiding deity. Rudra is a form of Shiva, whose mission is to destroy ignorance. He therefore directs the consciousness towards obtaining knowledge and finding the answers of life for ourselves. At Ardra we start to study or learn about the law of nature. It is the first time we become dissatisfied with the materialistic nature of our lives and start expanding towards differing horizons.

ARDRA AIM IS FOR KAMA
Kama motivates Ardra. Kama is desires and needs on a practical level. When we are born on this earth we have to have desires. Kama is passion – sexual, religious, for life, for a cause. Under Ardra the passion is for achievement: fulfilling impossible dreams and realizing inherent potentials.

GUNA TRIPLICITY: RAJAS, TAMAS AND SATTVA
The psychological quality of Ardra is expressed in the guna of Rajas on the primary (physical) level, Tamas on the secondary (mental) level and Sattva on the tertiary (spiritual) level. The three gunas reflected in Ardra show the importance of these psychological qualities in understanding the mind.

Outwardly Ardra is restless; tamasic mentality leads Ardra to get involved in ideas or relationships that block its path towards intellectual superiority. The subtle self is pure, showing the complete innocence and purity of Ardra soul.

AYURVEDIC DOSHA IS VATA
Ardra reflects the natural qualities of vata: action, agility and conflict. They are perceptive and inspirational. They are extremely active with lots of nervous energy to expend. Ardra have short attention spans and generally live on their nerves. They have to watch out for stress. They can be unrealistic and need to keep themselves grounded. Ardra are sociable people. Ardra love heat and warmth, and should avoid cold places.

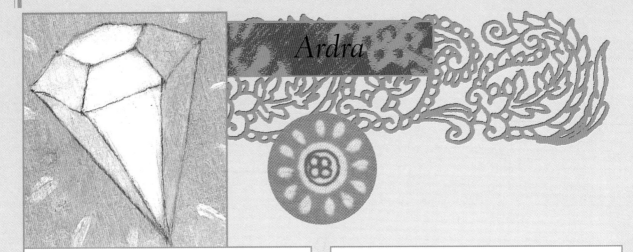

Ardra

CHARACTERISTICS/ PERSONALITY TRAITS

Ardra are successful and popular. They are always on the go. There is so much to do and experience that Ardra find themselves unable to decide. They have the ability to understand other points of view. At times they even neglect their own opinion. Ardra are sporty: they enjoy running, walking and flying. They are usually attracted to music, writing and acting. Computers are their allies.

Ardra have many friends. They like to gossip and party, and sometimes appear to be shallow. However, this would be a wrong judgement of Ardra. They are very deep and spiritual, but do not often reveal this part of their nature.

Ardra are ambitious – they need to be the best. Their ambitions can create conflict within themselves. They feel that by realizing their ambitions they will find happiness, but they are setting themselves up for disappointments.

Ardra need to access their deep spiritual self and try not to live life just in a superficial way. Sometimes they can make themselves deeply unhappy in the pursuit of excellence.

Ardra are the politicians of the zodiac. They know how to plan, manoeuvre, beguile, and play power games. However, their motivation is idealistic as revealed by their inner quality of Sattva.

They can never understand when others accuse them of being underhand or manipulative.

HOW IT LINKS WITH THE WESTERN SUN SIGN AND RULER

Ardra in Gemini: Those born on the cusp of Ardra can be in the end of Gemini. Being born at the end of Gemini and the beginning of Ardra is a karmic birth time. These people have a strong destiny ahead of them. They would make good politicians, writers and psychologists.

Ardra in Cancer: The Moon rules the Western sign and Rahu rules this nakshatra. These Ardras feel they are living within two worlds, the spiritual and the material. They are moving towards expressing themselves in this lifetime. These bright and intelligent people have a mysterious power surrounding them.

SPIRITUAL LIFE PATH

Ardra need to recognize their uniqueness, and learn to project their inner radiance for the good of others. Their karma is to express their knowledge for the good of this world. If they follow this path, they will be fulfilling their divine purpose. They possess a sharp and analytical mind.

RELATIONSHIPS

Ardra want the best relationship available to them. They are passionate, devoted and loving. They can sometimes give too much in their relationships. On the negative side, they can become dissatisfied with their partners for no good reason. Sometimes Ardra will sacrifice everything to fulfil their dream, only to realize that it was just an illusion. This is especially applicable to their relationships. They can break up a happy relationship to pursue another mate. This can often cause huge disappointment for Ardra, as they find the happiness offered by the new relationship is simply a mirage.

SEXUAL ENERGY LINKED TO THE FEMALE DOG

Ardra are sexually connected to the female dog. Female suggests passivity. Ardra will wait for their mates to make the first move. They may not necessary be faithful. They need a loving and caring partner. They will be constantly seeking approval. If Ardra are sexually attracted to someone, they will show their feelings immediately. They are open about their sexuality.

FAMOUS ARDRA

Princess Diana, George Orwell, Carl Lewis, George Michael, Meryl Streep.

HOW ARDRA RELATES TO OTHER NAKSHATRAS

Most compatible: Mrigasira, other Ardra, Swati, Purva Ashadha, Uttara Bhadra and Revati all relate well to Ardra. Mrigasira and other Ardra are intellectually exciting partners for them. Ardra find perfection in Swati, get excitement from Purva Ashadha, sensuality from Uttara Ashadha, and spiritual love from Revati.

Least compatible: Jyeshta is the most challenging nakshatra for Ardra. Both Ardra and Jyeshta consider themselves intellectually powerful, but differing intellectual paths create insurmountable obstacles. Jyeshta do not want to be contained by intellectual boundaries any longer, while Ardra wants to erect intellectual restrictions for itself so that it can learn from these limitations. Jyeshta and Ardra are pulled in different directions and it is very difficult for love to thrive in this situation.

Ideal sexual partner: Mula, the male dog, is the best sexual partner for Ardra. However, as the overall relationship between Mula and Ardra is only average, Ardra will have to look beyond a purely sexual relationship to find total compatibility with a partner.

Unsuitable sexual partners: The deer, Jyeshta and Anuradha, do not relate to Ardra sexually. Ardra, the dog, has a strong practical streak and the deer is a sensuous animal. Ardra's relationships with Jyeshta will always be extremely difficult, but Ardra and Anuradha can make a relationship work by learning to understand their different sexual personalities.

For complete relationships information see pages 128–139.

CUSPS

Those born at the end or beginning of the Ardra should check cusp details on page 140.

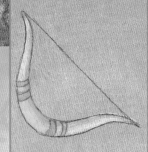

Punarvasu

5 July to 19 July

Key Words: Universal mother

Ruled by: Jupiter	
Symbol: Bow	
Animal sign: Cat	
Deity: Aditi, the goddess of infinity	
Motivation: Artha	
Guna triplicity: Rajas, Sattva, and Rajas	
Ayurvedic dosha: Vata	
Colour: Lead or steel grey	
Best direction: North	
Special consonants for birth names: Ke, Ko, Ha, Hi	
Principal stars: Geminorium	
Western signs: Cancer	

Symbol
Bow

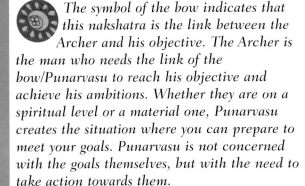

The symbol of the bow indicates that this nakshatra is the link between the Archer and his objective. The Archer is the man who needs the link of the bow/Punarvasu to reach his objective and achieve his ambitions. Whether they are on a spiritual level or a material one, Punarvasu creates the situation where you can prepare to meet your goals. Punarvasu is not concerned with the goals themselves, but with the need to take action towards them.

Meaning and Mythology

Punarvasu is situated in the sign of Cancer, which is ruled by the Moon. This nakshatra is ruled by Jupiter – the celestial guru who is there to guide us to our righteous path. Punarvasu deals with the transfer of knowledge from the spiritual to the earthly. Jupiter, as the true teacher, is responsible for guiding this process. Punarvasu deals with the mind's search for its true direction.

'Punarvasu' translates as 'Punah', meaning 'again', and 'Vasu' meaning 'brilliant', like rays of light. 'Vasu' also means 'to stay'. The full meaning of the nakshatra is to live simultaneously at different levels of cosmic manifestation.

Jupiter's rulership of this nakshatra and the Moon of the Western sign bring together wisdom and love. Jupiter guides us towards a new way of life, from our spiritual connection to the more material world. The Moon represents the mother in the zodiac, and also guides us through the difficult part of our life, from childhood to adult. This connection to guidance and trust is an important one for Punarvasu. Punarvasu therefore gives the individual the ability to be a trusted adviser and guide that others rely upon and trust. These people love unconditionally, in the same way that parents love their children.

Ruling deities

Punarvasu's ruling deity is Aditi who is the female principle, as well as the representation of infinity. Aditi is the Mother goddess of the Vedas. She is the mother of Adityas or the Sun gods. Aditya is the name of the Sun and Adityas is also the collective name for all the planets. She is identified with both heaven and earth – hence infinity.

PUNARVASU AIM IS FOR ARTHA

Artha motivates Punarvasu. Artha is the practical expression of life. Artha is goal-orientated. They want to create wealth, but it does not have to be on a purely material level. They may want to create wealth of knowledge, spirituality, or loving.

GUNAS TRIPLICITY: RAJAS, SATTVA AND RAJAS

The psychological quality of Punarvasu is expressed in the guna of Rajas on the primary (physical) level, Sattva on the secondary (mental) level and Rajas on the tertiary (spiritual) level. Punarvasu can be selfish as they concentrate on themselves and their restless search for truths. The other side of their personality is one that is always fighting for the rights of others. They are idealistic in their approach and pure in thought.

AYURVEDIC DOSHA IS VATA

Punarvasu are perceptive, enthusiastic and inspirational. They are extremely active with lots of nervous energy to expend. They have short attention spans and generally live on their nerves. They need constant mental stimulation and activity in order to keep interested. Punarvasu have a lower resistance to disease, and need warmth and comforting food in order to calm their over-excitable nature.

Punarvasu

CHARACTERISTICS/ PERSONALITY TRAITS

Punarvasu are caring and loving people. They will be constantly advising, guiding and nurturing others and have a fund of ideas. Punarvasu always need goals to achieve and ambitions to fulfil. Punarvasu must have a project, however small, or they will feel unsettled. This does not necessarily mean that they are great entrepreneurs.

Punarvasu need a large family. If they do not have a birth family, they will be naturally attracted to groups and associations where they can fulfil their mothering instincts. They have a great ability to connect to people at various levels. This means they usually have an extremely wide range of interests. They could be as happy making crafts as pursuing an interest in the occult.

They have an ability to get bored too easily and must try to keep their life interesting. Stillness and inactivity do not appeal. Taking part in sporting activities would be an excellent way of using up their surplus energy.

Although they are emotional, there is also an inner detachment. People can misunderstand Punarvasu's true nature. They relate to emotions and they can give a lot of love, but they remain detached, suddenly moving from the emotional self to the intellectual one.

One of the translations of their name is 'another home'. On a spiritual level, the soul finds another home to express itself, through its birth on earth. On a physical level, they travel from country to country or home to home. If this option is not available to Punarvasu, they can content themselves with re-decorating their home or reading about far-off places to fulfil their need for change.

HOW IT LINKS WITH THE WESTERN SUN SIGN AND RULER

Punarvasu in Cancer: The Moon rules your Western sign and Jupiter rules your nakshatra. Jupiter and Moon together reflect the combination of spiritual and earthly wisdom. Mental activities dominate Punarvasu. Jupiter makes you a natural teacher or adviser. Punarvasu are forever seeking the truth.

SPIRITUAL LIFE PATH

Punarvasu's spiritual life path is connected to the material life. Punarvasu's link to the eight vasus (who rule different levels of manifestation) gives them the ability to connect on different levels of consciousness. Punarvasu are forever trying to find the right surroundings for their soul to express itself properly.

RELATIONSHIPS

Punarvasu may not be happy loving just one person. They may be surrounded by people who want to be part of their lives. This can be very irritating for anyone who is in love with a Punarvasu, but they must have this expression. It is part of their karmic statement. To connect with people, to love them, nurture them, and guide them towards a better future is Punarvasu's spiritual role. They are not necessarily being unfaithful to their partners. They are expressing their love for the human race through guidance and advice.

SEXUAL ENERGY LINKED TO THE FEMALE CAT

Punarvasu's connection to cat sexuality shows their independence. They do not like others trying to control them. Although they may be surrounded by the opposite sex, they are loners. Punarvasu is the female cat; therefore they will be slow in expressing their sexual desires. They may appear proud and detached. If they take a fancy to someone, they will send out subtle signals: the odd caress, perhaps, to test the waters. Potential mates will need to be very aware to understand these subtle messages. They wait for others to take the first steps to establish contact.

FAMOUS PUNARVASU

Richard Branson, Harrison Ford, Rembrandt, Robert the Bruce of Scotland, W.G. Grace.

HOW PUNARVASU RELATES TO OTHER NAKSHATRAS

Most compatible: Bharani and Pushya are the best nakshatras for Punarvasu. Punarvasu know how to keep Bharani's passions burning and their varied and exciting life fascinates Bharani. Punarvasu bring out the best in shy Pushya, while Pushya support and love Punarvasu. Punarvasu find Swati fascinating, and Uttara Bhadra rewarding.

Least compatible: Punarvasu tries to understand Jyeshta's complex personality. Jyeshta sees through Punarvasu's need to be universally loved, and will challenge them intellectually at every opportunity. Punarvasu find it easier to walk away from relationships with Jyeshta rather than try to work them out. Shatabhishak are too mysterious; they are never able to let Punarvasu into their secret needs and desires. Punarvasu may love them superficially, but a deeper connection is almost impossible to establish.

Ideal sexual partner: Ashlesha, the male cat, is the best sexual partner for Punarvasu. The overall relationship between Ashlesha and Punarvasu is also good, indicating that Punarvasu can find fulfilment from their animal counterpart.

Unsuitable sexual partners: The worst sexual partner for the cat Punarvasu is their natural enemy the rat, Magha and Purva Phalguni. Rats like sex unembellished and cats like it to be full of sensuality and passion. Their sexual needs have no common ground and there is a hidden danger in this relationship of a predator and its prey. In the end Punarvasu can become too strong and sexually powerful.

For complete relationships information see pages 128–139.

CUSPS

Those born at the end or beginning of Punarvasu should check the cusp details on pages 140–141.

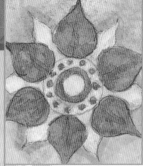

Pushya

19 JULY TO 2 AUGUST

Key Words: Fragrant and colourful

Ruled by: Saturn

Symbol: Flower, arrow and circle

Animal sign: Sheep

Deity: Brihaspati

Motivation: Dharma

Guna triplicity: Rajas, Sattva and Tamas

Ayurvedic dosha: Pitta

Colour: Red and black

Best direction: East

Special consonants for birth names: Hoo, He, Ho, Da

Principal stars: An-Nathrah

Western signs: Cancer (19 to 23 July) and Leo (24 July to 2 August)

Meaning and Mythology

'Pushya' means to 'nourish' or 'thrive'. Pushya work to nourish others and create conditions in which the world can thrive. Pushya is considered a very auspicious nakshatra.

Pushya is placed at the ending of Cancer and the beginning of Leo. The two luminaries, the Moon and the Sun, rule these signs respectively. The ruler of Pushya is Saturn. The connection of Saturn with the two luminaries shows the profound impact of life on individuals born in Pushya. Saturn teaches us about responsibility, death and transformations, so that we can search for our true light. Saturn's relationship with these luminaries is a difficult one. Saturn makes us aware of karma that has to be faced on earth. Facing this karma leads to personal development and strength.

Pushya's presiding deity is Brihaspati, another name for Jupiter. It is an expansive planet; increasing everything it touches. Saturn, the planet that brings forth karmic restrictions, is the ruler of this nakshatra. These dual influences are what make Pushya so special. A balance between expansion and restriction is achieved. The soul's restrictions as well as its knowledge of its limitlessness are fully expressed under Pushya. At the stage of Pushya, the soul understands that this life is only part of a whole – not the whole itself.

Symbol
FLOWER

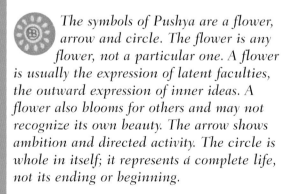

The symbols of Pushya are a flower, arrow and circle. The flower is any flower, not a particular one. A flower is usually the expression of latent faculties, the outward expression of inner ideas. A flower also blooms for others and may not recognize its own beauty. The arrow shows ambition and directed activity. The circle is whole in itself; it represents a complete life, not its ending or beginning.

Ruling deities

Pushya's presiding deity is Brihaspati, which is another name for Jupiter. Brihaspati is the primary priest in the Vedas and adviser to the gods. Brihaspati teaches wisdom and love of truth. His work is for the good of humanity. Brihaspati advises the gods on their religious duties and purification rituals that are needed for a sattvic life. He is also considered to be the founder of Vedic religion.

PUSHYA AIM IS FOR DHARMA

Dharma motivates Pushya. Responsibility, doing the right thing, duty to themselves, their family and the world dominate the thoughts of Pushya. They will always aim to do what is correct, and are never shy of facing up to their responsibilities, however hard they may be.

GUNA TRIPLICITY: RAJAS, SATTVA AND TAMAS

The psychological quality of Punarvasu is expressed in the guna of Rajas on the primary (physical) level, Sattva on the secondary (mental) level and Tamas on the tertiary (spiritual) level. There is a restless search for self-expression and the mind desires calmness and peace. Tamas at the spiritual level indicates the soul has to express itself on an earthly plane.

AYURVEDIC DOSHA IS PITTA

Pushya reflects the dosha of pitta, the fiery quality. Pushya are intelligent, spirited and warm. They are decisive and action-orientated. They are creative, knowledgeable and intelligent. They have a tendency to burn out quickly. They need to calm their temperament with cool colours, food and places.

Pushya

CHARACTERISTICS/ PERSONALITY TRAITS

Pushya may be weighed down by their responsibilities. They are hardworking and creative, with lots of ideas, and have the ability to turn their ideas into reality. They must have an objective to work towards, and if they plan their career, they can be extremely successful. Knowledge and its expression is the most important aspect of Pushya's personality.

They do not always recognize their own qualities. Like the flower that symbolizes their nakshatra, they bloom and use their creativity for the good of others. They will be fragrant, beautiful and colourful, but have a tendency to wilt quickly, so they need to look after themselves. Calmness and tranquillity will help them to relax and rejuvenate.

Pushya are often in conflict with themselves. People may accuse them of not being true to their principles. This is not correct. Pushya recognize their own inner purity and eternal connection, but accept that they have to work on a practical, worldly level. They struggle with these varying shades of their personality, and often confuse others at the same time. They have a great ability to tolerate pain. They will face adversity with equanimity. This can sometimes keep them in unhappy situations for longer than is necessary.

On a negative level, Pushya can become too dogmatic, restrictive and fundamentalist. Their fear of expansion can make them unable to express fully their own creativity.

HOW IT LINKS WITH THE WESTERN SUN SIGN AND RULER

Pushya in Cancer: The Moon rules the Western sign and Saturn rules this nakshatra. The Moon is changeable; Saturn is rigid and restrictive. The Moon learns the important lesson of control, and Saturn learns the lesson of change.

Pushya in Leo: The Sun rules Leo and Saturn rules this nakshatra. Saturn stops the full expressions of solar energy. The Sun/Saturn combination produces a great sense of duty and destiny. The influence of the Sun and Saturn on Pushya makes for a formidable combination.

SPIRITUAL LIFE PATH

Pushya are spiritually connected to doing the right thing. They must express themselves through work, responsibility and duty. Pushya need to understand duty to themselves as well as to others. The spiritual path they adopt is to work within their given karma. Religion and philosophy will enable them to overcome their inner conflicts.

HOW PUSHYA RELATES TO OTHER NAKSHATRAS

Most compatible: Ashwini and Ashlesha are the best nakshatras for Pushya. Pushya are attracted to Ashwini's independence and courage. Ashlesha know how to romance Pushya, and they connect spiritually and emotionally. Pushya find Rohini exciting, Punarvasu loving, other Pushya understanding, and Revati spiritually invigorating.

Least compatible: Chitra and Dhanishta are the most difficult nakshatras for Pushya to deal with. Pushya find Chitra's energy and verve difficult to handle. Pushya will always try to mould Chitra into their own image. Dhanishta are too idealistic; Pushya can develop an inferiority complex trying to live up to their standards of perfection. In fact, appreciating what the other has to bring into the relationship and allowing each other space would go a long way towards defusing any tensions within the relationship.

Ideal sexual partner: Pushya, the ram, connects passionately to the female sheep, Krittika. Pushya also relates well with Krittika in all areas of life, so these are good partnerships – sexually satisfying and emotionally complete.

Unsuitable sexual partners: Purva Ashadha and Shravana, the monkeys, are sexually incompatible with Pushya. Pushya like to pursue their partners; they are possessive. Monkeys do not want to be either captured or possessed. They will tease and manipulate Pushya, never making a commitment. Pushya sometimes lack the finesse and sensuality that the monkeys want.

For complete relationship information, see pages 128–139.

CUSPS

Those born at the end or beginning of the Pushya should check the cusp details on page 141.

RELATIONSHIPS

Pushya are self-contained and want their partners to be so. Pushya find it difficult to express their inner feelings, even to those they love. Their partners often misunderstand them, as they do not explain or project what they feel. They need to overcome their shyness, otherwise their partners could end up feeling unwanted.

Pushya may feel they are carrying the burden of the world on their shoulders. As they are good advisers, people will seek them out.

They are strong and make good friends, but they have high expectations from their friends and may not accept them if they show human weaknesses.

SEXUAL ENERGY LINKED TO THE MALE SHEEP

Sheep like to be part of the herd. They are skittish and playful. They will flee from, rather than fight for their mate. The male sexuality shows an active side of Pushya. They need to be in control of their sexuality. Both sexes of Pushya like to pursue their partners. Potential mates should try not to make them jealous. However much Pushya are attracted to someone, they will not fight for them. Sex needs to be fun for them; they seldom make long-term commitments.

FAMOUS PUSHYA

Sir Edmund Hillary, Ernest Hemingway, Raymond Chandler, Beatrix Potter, Henry Ford.

Ashlesha

2 AUGUST TO 16 AUGUST

Key Word: Hypnotic

Ruled by:	Mercury
Symbol:	Serpent
Animal sign:	Cat
Deity:	Nagas
Motivation:	Dharma
Guna triplicity:	Rajas, Sattva and Sattva
Ayurvedic dosha:	Kapha
Colour:	Red and black
Best direction:	South
Special consonants for birth names:	De, Doo, Day, Do
Principal stars:	Hydarae
Western signs:	Leo

Meaning and Mythology

'Ashlesha' means 'to embrace'. Ashlesha is wholly in Leo. It indicates the soul embracing life so that it can act out its karma. This nakshatra is extremely powerful on a spiritual level, and destiny plays an important part. As soon as we embrace life, we are subject to the rules and regulations of the earth. Our life becomes involved in the process of life and death, happiness and unhappiness. Destiny, born from our own actions in previous lives, influences our present lifetime.

The ruler of Ashlesha is Mercury, the celestial bridge between higher forces and the earth. It is also the intellect, the ego within humans, which makes them different from other animals. Mercury, as the ego, identifies an individual from the universal soul. The Sun, Leo's ruler, is the soul. Mercury guides our rational thinking. This focuses Ashlesha on the development of the human mind and the changes in psyche that take place when we are born on earth.

The connection of Ashlesha to the Nagas, the celestial snakes, links them to wisdom. They radiate mystical powers which can bring enlightenment. However, if wrongly used these powers can be dangerous.

Symbol
SERPENT

The serpents signify wisdom in the Vedas. The serpent here is the king Cobra. All Vedic/Indian gods pay homage to the serpents. There will always be a serpent symbol with the gods: they serve to remind humans of their mortality. The serpent shedding its skin is a symbol of rebirth and transformation. This process is always a painful one. It relates to changes of the mind: emotional and intellectual, and the evolving of human consciousness.

The Kundalini power that the serpents represent when fully aroused can bring spiritual enlightenment and occult powers.

HOW ASHLESHA RELATES TO OTHER NAKSHATRAS

Most compatible: Pushya are the best nakshatras for Ashlesha. Pushya's dependability and love provides steadiness in Ashlesha's often tumultuous life. Ashlesha also connect deeply with Ashwini; Ashlesha feel that Ashwini is leading a life that projects their desires. Together they can make a difference to the world. Ashlesha feel connected in a deeply spiritual way to other Ashlesha; there is a karmic link as well as an emotional one.

Least compatible: Uttara Ashadha is the nakshatra Ashlesha will have most difficulty connecting to. The mongoose rules Uttara Ashadha. Ashlesha's ruling deity is the nagas or serpents, and its symbol is also the serpent. The mongoose and serpents are deadly enemies in nature. This relationship is inimical on a subtle level, and they are emotionally unable to fulfil the other's requirements. This relationship has the potential to develop very negatively.

Ideal sexual partner: Punarvasu, the female cat, is the best sexual partner for Ashlesha. Ashlesha and Punarvasu relate well to each other in other areas of life, making this partnership sexually exciting as well as emotionally happy.

Unsuitable sexual partners: The worst sexual partners for Ashleshas are their natural enemies, the rats – Magha and Purva Phalguni. Ashlesha are sexually demanding and although the rats like sex, they are usually unimaginative and straightforward. As natural enemies, this relationship does not take long to move from emotional passion to sexual rivalry. *For complete relationship information see pages 128–139.*

CUSPS

Those born at the end or beginning of the Ashlesha should check the cusp details on page 141.

RELATIONSHIPS

Ashlesha are self-contained and need relationships that allow them their independence. They will be possessive, but do not like others to be possessive with them. They like to feel that they are the centre of their partner's universe, or they can become cold and distant.

Ashlesha are the glamorous people of the zodiac. They may have many admirers, but find it difficult to express themselves in one-to-one relationships.

SEXUAL ENERGY LINKED TO THE MALE CAT

Ashlesha are sensuous, manipulative and independent. They want to suit themselves. They can be aggressive if anyone tries to make them adhere to their rules. They may be haughty and proud, and will only lavish attention on their mates when they feel like it, which can make them selfish lovers.

Although they will often be surrounded by the opposite sex, underneath, Ashlesha are loners. The best way to love them is to allow them their independence. They may be jealous of their partner's relationships with others; but the same rules do not apply to them. Ashlesha can be loving, sensuous and committed if their partner accepts them as they are.

FAMOUS ASHLESHA
Alfred Hitchcock, Mata Hari, Robert Mitchum, Enid Blyton, Madonna.

Magha

16 AUGUST TO 30 AUGUST

Key Words: Fame and power

Ruled by: Ketu	
Symbol: Palanquin	
Animal sign: Rat	
Deity: Pitris, the forefathers	
Motivation: Artha	
Guna triplicity: Tamas, Rajas and Rajas	
Ayurvedic dosha: Kapha	
Colour: Ivory or cream	
Best direction: West	
Special consonants for birth names: Ma, Me, Moo, May	
Principal stars: Regulus	
Western signs: Leo (16 to 23 August) and Virgo (24 to 30 August)	

Meaning and Mythology

Magha is the second nakshatra ruled by Ketu. Magha is partly in the sign of Leo, ruled by the Sun, and partly in Virgo, ruled by Mercury. The Leo/Magha combination strongly emphasizes power, royalty, courage, strong intellect, ambition and aspiration to limitless success. In the Virgo/Magha combination, the intellect dominates. The focus is on the mind and the development of intellectual power. The abilities of all Magha are linked to their past life karma. They will enjoy worldly pleasures because of the actions of past lives.

'Magha' means 'mighty' or 'great'. People born in this nakshatra aspire towards eminence and are usually prominent in their chosen field.

Magha is the beginning of the second cycle in the soul's journey. The signs Leo to Scorpio indicate the soul's full involvement in the pleasures and pains of earthly life. Tamas represents illusion, darkness and attachment. Ketu, as the significator of spiritual realization, rules the starting point of the materialistic journey, which shows the importance of experiencing the realities of life whilst fulfilling the divine mission of the soul.

Magha are idealistic even if their mission is to fulfil their materialistic needs; this can create misunderstandings at times. Others suspect their honour and sincerity. Magha give a lot materially, but they know intuitively that the material happiness is only an experience; they still need to follow the inner purpose of life and move towards moksha.

Symbol
PALANQUIN

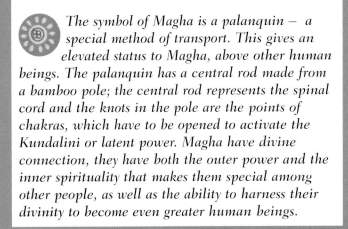

The symbol of Magha is a palanquin – a special method of transport. This gives an elevated status to Magha, above other human beings. The palanquin has a central rod made from a bamboo pole; the central rod represents the spinal cord and the knots in the pole are the points of chakras, which have to be opened to activate the Kundalini or latent power. Magha have divine connection, they have both the outer power and the inner spirituality that makes them special among other people, as well as the ability to harness their divinity to become even greater human beings.

Ruling deities

Magha's ruling deity is Pitris, the fathers of humanity, whose mission is to guide their children to the right course of life. The fathers only interfere if the individual is straying from the right path. Pitris makes the sign of Magha very auspicious. They always have great power to guide them through even the most difficult times of life.

MAGHA AIM IS FOR ARTHA

Artha or practical expression of life motivates Magha. Magha is the second level of the soul's development. Its motivation as artha indicates that the material expression of life – being successful, happy and rich – is as important as the spiritual one.

GUNAS TRIPLICITY: TAMAS, RAJAS AND RAJAS

This is the first time Tamas becomes the primary psychological force. Magha's expression of the guna of Tamas on the primary (physical) level, Rajas on the secondary (mental) level and tertiary (spiritual) level indicates that Magha is still searching for answers within, while its outer personality is involved in the practical and material aspects of life. This inner conflict creates restlessness within Magha; their inner spirit remains dissatisfied, regardless of their outer achievements.

AYURVEDIC DOSHA IS KAPHA

Magha is kapha. They are emotional, calm and philosophical. Magha's kapha dosha makes them appear calmer than they really are. They have large frames and a tendency to put on weight, sometimes as a result of comfort eating. When Magha feel under extreme stress, they resort to food.

Magha

CHARACTERISTICS/ PERSONALITY TRAITS

Magha are special people. Their radiance attracts many admirers and friends. They are clever and intelligent and are enterprising people who will be leaders of their community. Magha are attracted to power; if they are not already in a position of power, they will aspire to one. Magha will be very frustrated if they are not given their due importance.

Community is important to Magha. They will try to do worthy deeds for the good of all, not simply for their own glory. This can make them good politicians, leaders and entrepreneurs. They lead with kindness and silent strength, which makes them universally popular, but can also cause jealousy and create hidden enemies. Magha need to be careful about whom they trust.

Magha are conservative and traditional. They can also be cautious, obstinate and old-fashioned. They respect others and will never deliberately try to hurt someone. They are dependable, caring and pleasant and love life. They enjoy food and partying; and make wonderful hosts. On the negative side, Magha can be arrogant and hot-tempered. This can block their personal growth. Magha must be careful not to try to play god.

HOW IT LINKS WITH THE WESTERN SUN SIGN AND RULER

Magha in Leo: The Sun/Ketu connection indicates both power and humility. Magha in Leo can be intensely powerful, but they will always remember their roots. They will be just, kind and sensitive. Magha enjoy the good things in life, but they have a strong connection to the spiritual, too.

Magha in Virgo: The Mercury/Ketu combination is easier. Mercury understands both its spiritual connection and its earthly role. Magha born under this sign will be more comfortable with themselves. They aspire to intellectual success and will feel unfulfilled if their intellectual powers are not recognized.

SPIRITUAL LIFE PATH

Magha need to externalize their inherent capabilities. Their qualities have to come out so that they can do good for the community and guide other souls towards their right path, while retaining their own humility. Much wisdom has been gathered through the actions of past lives. Now they are being given an opportunity to bring forth the results. Magha's spiritual path is connected to doing the right thing in this earthly lifetime.

RELATIONSHIPS

Magha get great enjoyment from their love life. Their problem is finding a suitable mate: Magha have an idealistic vision of their partner, which means they have to search long and hard to find the right person. Magha may lead full and busy lives, but find they are lonely among other people. Magha women are very strong and usually have a good career; they were doing this before it became the norm. They are not stay-at-home types at all. They need partners who understand their need for strength and power.

SEXUAL ENERGY LINKED TO THE MALE RAT

Magha develop their sexuality early and enjoy sex. The male energy of the rat means they will actively pursue and woo unwilling partners. This is a very virile sign and they should be especially careful with contraception.

Magha are always ready for sex. They may enjoy multiple couplings in a sexual encounter. This voracious sexual appetite can be tiring for those who are not equally sensuous. Remember that if you do not satisfy your Magha partner, they will look elsewhere to satisfy their needs.

FAMOUS MAGHA

Bill Clinton, Roman Polanski, Claude Debussy, Gene Kelly, Ingrid Bergman, Leo Tolstoy.

HOW MAGHA RELATES TO OTHER NAKSHATRAS

Most compatible: In Jyeshta, Magha find an ideal partner – intelligent, witty and charming, with a hint of mystery. There will always be an exciting edge to this relationship. Purva Phalguni will also make intensely satisfying relationships for Magha, connecting sexually and emotionally.

Least compatible: Uttara Ashadha is the most difficult relationship for Magha. It can become a relationship of power struggles and emotional rivalry. Each is trying to be in control, but neither is willing to compromise to make their relationship work. If this relationship stands any chance of success, they will both have to be more flexible. Shravana is another difficult one. Magha have a tendency to reject Shravana or make them feel unwanted.

Ideal sexual partner: Magha, the male rat, connects best with the female rat, Purva Phalguni. Magha and Purva Phalguni both enjoy sex, and need lots of it to keep them satisfied. In other areas these two are also compatible, so this relationship has the potential to be a match made in heaven.

Unsuitable sexual partners: The worst sexual partners for Magha, the Rat, are their natural enemies, the cats – Ashlesha and Punarvasu. Magha may find themselves being dominated sexually. As natural enemies, a relationship between them will take a short time to move from ardour to antagonism.

For complete relationship information see pages 128–139.

CUSPS

Those born at the end or beginning of the Magha should check the cusp details on page 141.

Purva Phalguni

30 August to 13 September

Key Words: Creativity and good luck

Ruled by: Venus	
Symbol: Fireplace	
Animal sign: Rat	
Deity: Bhaga, the Vedic god of luck	
Motivation: Kama	
Guna triplicity: Tamas, Rajas and Tamas	
Ayurvedic dosha: Pitta	
Colour: Pale brown	
Best direction: North	
Special consonants for birth names: Mo, Ta, Tee, Too	
Principal stars: Az-Zubrah.	
Western signs: Virgo.	

Meaning and Mythology

Purva Phalguni and Uttara Phalguni are two parts of a whole nakshatra of four stars, which resemble a bed. They indicate similar purposes but have very specific differences. Purva Phalguni is entirely in the sign of Virgo, ruled by Mercury. It is ruled by Venus, the planet that rules the good things in life. Venus and Mercury are good friends in the zodiac, and together they make this nakshatra very productive. 'Phal' means 'fruit' and 'guni' means 'connected to gunas or good qualities'. Phalguni is the nakshatra that gives the fruit of our good deeds. Purva means west, indicating that it is the western part of the Phalguni nakshatras. This nakshatra has the capacity to fulfil our desires on a materialistic level.

The Mercury/Venus combination gives abundant wealth and happiness. Mercury, as the intellect, takes time out from its search for answers to relax a bit, to allow itself to be distracted by its friend Venus, and to enjoy the pleasures of life. Bhaga, the presiding deity of Purva Phalguni, is another name for the Sun, thus adding solar beneficence to this nakshatra and magnifying its results for the good. This is the nakshatra for achievement, enjoying the fruits of past actions on a material level, and Purva Phalguni is the nakshatra where the desire for children is very pronounced.

Symbol

the Fireplace

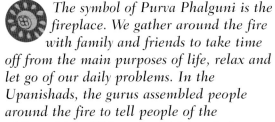

The symbol of Purva Phalguni is the fireplace. We gather around the fire with family and friends to take time off from the main purposes of life, relax and let go of our daily problems. In the Upanishads, the gurus assembled people around the fire to tell people of the philosophies of life and enlighten their thoughts. Higher thoughts and pleasures of life are all intermingled in Purva Phalguni.

Ruling deities

The ruling deity Bhaga, the god of good fortune and luck, indicates that the fruits promised by Purva Phalguni are usually highly auspicious. Indian philosophy believes that good luck shines on you as a result of the actions of your past life. Bhaga is a Sun god; he is one of the 12 sons of Aditi, the universal mother. Bhaga also stands for a woman's womb and procreation. It is considered good luck for a woman if she bears children.

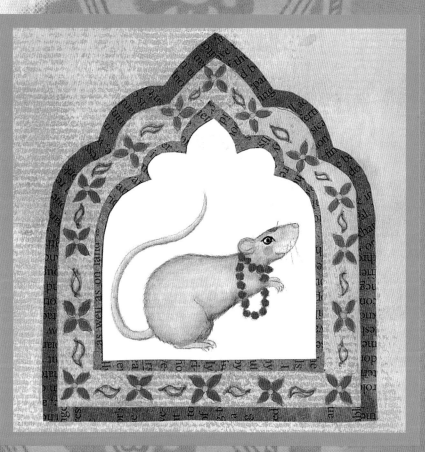

PURVA PHALGUNI AIM IS FOR KAMA

Under Purva Phalguni, the passion is for children, family, friends, creativity and enjoying life. The desire for a close family unit and the success of their children motivate Purva Phalguni. Those who do not have children will focus their passion on their creativity and ideas.

GUNA TRIPLICITY: TAMAS, RAJAS AND TAMAS

The psychological quality of Purva Phalguni on a primary (physical) level and tertiary (spiritual) level is Tamas, and Rajas on the secondary (mental) level. The involvement in Tamas shows the soul is immersed in the web of desires. The soul is happy in the material world where it is creating its attachments, but the mind is still restless and not totally happy in this purely material world.

AYURVEDIC DOSHA IS PITTA

Purva Phalguni reflects the dosha of pitta, the fiery quality. Purva Phalguni are warm and loving. They are creative, knowledgeable and intelligent. They are passionate and sensuous. They are ambitious and they work very hard to achieve their desires. Purva Phalguni need to be careful as they have a tendency to burn out quickly. They are vital and aggressive. They need kapha or vata partners who can absorb their intensity and fire.

Purva Phalguni

CHARACTERISTICS/ PERSONALITY TRAITS

Purva Phalguni tend to be lucky. They are charismatic, charming and warm. They work hard and enjoy life. Their vital personalities attract success. This can bring them into the public domain and further highlight their success.

Both sexes of Purva Phalguni are very fond of children and make good parents. Children are seen as divine creativity and their birth gives the ability for a human to harness this natural power. Establishing a family unit and perpetuating humanity are important to Purva Phalguni.

Purva Phalguni always seem to get things more easily than others. Most people experience many ups and downs in life, but for Purva Phalguni these negative periods are not so intense. They do not make a song and dance about mishaps and setbacks, and ensure they get the most out of the positive periods of life.

They are sincere and truthful. They try to do the right thing. They are often the life and soul of the party. They enjoy making money as it helps to make life more comfortable. Purva Phalguni have excellent taste: their homes will be comfortable and sensuous.

They enjoy power and authority. They like to work in an environment where they are completely appreciated. They are not worried about disagreeing with popular opinion, even if it is shared by their seniors or bosses.

HOW IT LINKS WITH THE WESTERN SUN SIGN AND RULER

Purva Phalguni in Virgo: Mercury and Venus relate well to each other. Mercury understands both its spiritual connection and its earthly role. People of this sign express and enjoy their material role. They want to achieve both intellectually and materially to make an impact on life. Their aim for excellence is so that they can live life in comfort, surrounded by family and friends.

SPIRITUAL LIFE PATH

Purva Phalguni's spiritual path is connected to children and creativity, enjoying the fruits of their labour, creating karma through children and being involved in every aspect of life. Purva Phalguni should enjoy life, but remember that there is a higher karma to experience at a later date. The soul has been given special dispensation to enjoy life to the full.

RELATIONSHIPS

Purva Phalguni generally have good relationships. They want long-term committed partnerships, and they will make sacrifices to keep them. Children are an important part of Purva Phalguni relationships and they are willing to sacrifice a lot for their children. In the rare cases where a Purva Phalguni relationship goes wrong, they will remain very attached to their children. If Purva Phalguni do not have children as a common binding force, then other shared interests will be important. Pursuing common creative goals with a partner will keep their relationship alive.

SEXUAL ENERGY LINKED TO THE FEMALE RAT

Purva Phalguni develop their sexuality early and they enjoy sex. It is a virile and fertile sign, strongly connected to the birth of children, so they should be careful to use contraception.

Purva Phalguni will wait until they are wooed. However, if they are interested in someone, they will send out covert signals as part of a mating dance. If you are interested in Purva Phalguni, do not be put off by their rudeness or anger. They enjoy a good fight – it is their way of arousing passion.

FAMOUS PURVA PHALGUNI

Jimmy Connors, Buddy Holly, Raquel Welch, Antonin Dvorák, Patsy Cline, Barry Gibb.

HOW PURVA PHALGUNI RELATES TO OTHER NAKSHATRAS

Most compatible: A relationship with Magha will be the most harmonious for Purva Phalguni, making them feel happy, sexually satisfied and emotionally complete. Other Purva Phalguni also bring happiness through children and close family love. Uttara Phalguni may be soulmates. Both nakshatras need family ties and bonds, and love for their children will keep them bound together forever.

Least compatible: Chitra and Dhanishta are the most difficult nakshatras for Purva Phalguni to connect with. Mars rules these nakshatras and Purva Phalguni's ruler is Venus. Mars and Venus together create passion, but once this dies down, there is usually not much left to build the foundations of a long-term relationship.

Ideal sexual partner: Purva Phalguni, the female rat, connects well with the male rat, Magha. Magha and Purva Phalguni are creatures with large sexual appetites. They recognize each other's sensuous desires. They are also very compatible in other areas; this relationship therefore works beyond the merely sexual.

Unsuitable sexual partners: The worst sexual partners for the rat, Purva Phalguni, are their natural enemies, the cats – Ashlesha and Punarvasu. Cats will always try to dominate Purva Phalguni. There may be excitement to start with, but as there is a lack of real sexual compatibility, this relationship can become bland and unhappy.
For complete relationship information see pages 128–139.

CUSPS

Those born at the end or beginning of the Purva Phalguni should check the cusp details on page 141.

Uttara Phalguni

13 SEPTEMBER TO 26 SEPTEMBER

Key Words: Struggles with destiny

Ruled by: The Sun

Symbol: Four legs of the bed

Animal sign: Bull

Deity: Aryaman

Motivation: Moksha

Guna triplicity: Tamas, Rajas and Sattva

Ayurvedic dosha: Vata

Colour: Bright blue

Best direction: East

Special consonants for birth names:
Tay, Too, Pa, Pe

Principal stars: Al Sarfah

Western signs: Virgo (13 to 23 September) and Libra (24 to 26 September)

Symbol
FOUR LEGS OF A BED

The four legs of the bed represent the sexual energy of the soul, the downward flow of the power. Each of the legs represents the sheaths in which the soul becomes entangled – the physical, the ethereal, the astral and the mental. These sheaths surround the evolving soul during its stay in the Phalgunis. The number four also represents the four heads of Brahma, the four directions, and the four Vedas.

Meaning and Mythology

Purva Phalguni and Uttara Phalguni are two parts of a whole nakshatra of four stars, which resemble a bed. They indicate similar purposes but have very specific differences. It is the other half of the picture – the male energy to Purva's female. 'Phal' means 'fruit' and 'guni' means 'connected to gunas or good qualities'. 'Uttara' means 'east', indicating it is the eastern part of the Phalguni nakshatras. This nakshatra has the capacity to fulfil our desires on a materialistic level.

Uttara Phalguni is partly in Virgo (Mercury) and partly in Libra (Venus). Virgo is the sign for service, and Libra for justice. Uttara Phalguni is ruled by the Sun, the ruler of the universe, the significator of authority and power. In Uttara Phalguni, the Sun is all-powerful as the ruler of the nakshatra. The deity of Uttara Phalguni, Aryaman, is another Sun god. The Sun signifies creation and carries within it the knowledge of individual karma.

Uttara Phalguni allows the soul to recognize its own failings as well as the restrictions imposed on it by its limited destiny in this life. They work for perfection, maturity of the soul, and the ripening of their 'fruit', so that the soul can break away from its purely material role. But their happiness lies in being reconciled with their material goal, not struggling against it.

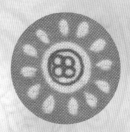

Ruling deities

Aryaman is another solar god who is the son of Aditi, the universal mother. He is famous for his leadership qualities. As a nakshatra it bestows those qualities on an incarnating soul as well as allowing it to recognize that his ambitions are limited by the vastness of the task ahead. He gives courage in the face of adversity, individual effort against all odds.

UTTARA PHALGUNI AIM IS FOR MOKSHA

Uttara Phalguni is the nakshatra that reflects complete involvement in the material aspects of life. However, its motivation of moksha reveals that this involvement is not enough for Uttara Phalguni and they recognize the bigger picture. Their ruler, the Sun, represents the eternal connection and it helps Uttara Phalguni to move towards moksha while still reaping the rewards of its karma.

GUNA TRIPLICITY: TAMAS, RAJAS AND SATTVA

The psychological quality of Uttara Phalguni is Tamas on a primary (physical) level, Rajas on the secondary (mental) level and Sattva on the tertiary (spiritual) level. Outwardly, Uttara Phalguni is involved in enjoying the fruits of life, but mentally there is a restless search for something more. The spirit is pure. They know the innocence of their spiritual self and will always remain true to it.

AYURVEDIC DOSHA IS VATA

Uttara Phalguni's dosha is vata, but their nervousness may not be immediately apparent. They look placid and calm from the outside, but they will become vata when things do not work out as they should. They can live on their nerves and can get stressed quickly. Uttara Phalguni need to have well-planned schedules. They need security and stability. Sudden changes in their life can make them ill.

Uttara Phalguni

CHARACTERISTICS/ PERSONALITY TRAITS

Uttara Phalguni are giving people. They desire to give to other individuals, their community and their country. They are friendly and warm, charismatic and attractive. They lead by example. They are ambitious and have a great capacity for hard work. Like their animal sign, the bull, they can carry out boring tasks such as tilling the soil for planting new seeds. The bull is also considered a symbol of fertility, and these people are virile, strong and courageous.

Uttara Phalguni are good planners and strategists, which means they can be good politicians. They may always appear to be reliable, but when you get close to them you will find that their insecurities and tensions can make them act in a completely different way. They are usually steadfast and dependable if they have a focused direction. However, they can lack confidence in their own power and abilities, making them nervous, restless and unsure.

HOW IT LINKS WITH THE WESTERN SUN SIGN AND RULER

Uttara Phalguni in Virgo: Solar power added to the mercurial desires of Virgo, make this part of Uttara Phalguni prominent in analysing the goals of life and acting on them. They are responsible, idealistic and hard-working. They should try to be more realistic about life. Virgo represents service and Uttara Phalguni stands for directed activity. These two need to work towards achieving the chosen goals.

Uttara Phalguni in Libra: Libra is about balancing the spiritual and the material, while Uttara Phalguni is about ambition and power. As Libra Phalguni learn to bring some kind of balance into life, and are more able to understand their restrictions, they will try to make their lives happier. They may be idealistic, but they're also realistic. They find it easier to deal with life on the material level.

SPIRITUAL LIFE PATH

Uttara Phalguni directs the soul to its earthbound role. The individual becomes a conduit through which the soul can express its earthly karma. Their spiritual life path is connected to fulfilling this responsibility properly. They need immense courage and warrior spirit to express this karma as they experience the trials and tribulations of life. This is never easy, but the experiences of life allow the soul to mature and prepare for the next level of spiritual growth.

RELATIONSHIPS

Uttara Phalguni need relationships. At times their perfectionist streak can create problems, as they will reject relationships that they consider less than perfect. They often make a practical marriage, even though this goes against their natural instincts to find a perfect relationship. As a result, they are hard on themselves and their partners. They have an independent spirit, but part of them desires to be part of a family group. They are natural givers in relationships; and will be there for their partners. In return they want appreciation and love.

SEXUAL ENERGY LINKED TO THE BULL

This is a very vital sign connected to Shiva's Nandi bull, the symbol of divine virility, which is prayed to by Indian women for fertility. Indians believe that sexuality should be expressed within committed relationships and should bear positive results (children).

The greatest challenge to anyone in love with Uttara Phalguni is to keep them interested sexually. Uttara Phalguni need partners who will not give in to them too easily. If they feel they have to chase their mates, it will keep them interested. They want commitment, but when they get it, they can become bored.

FAMOUS UTTARA PHALGUNI

Agatha Christie, Lauren Bacall, Greta Garbo, Sophia Lauren, Bruce Springsteen, F. Scott Fitzgerald.

HOW UTTARA PHALGUNI RELATES TO OTHER NAKSHATRAS

Most compatible: Purva Phalguni and Anuradha are the best nakshatras for Uttara Phalguni. They are astronomically connected to each other, but emotionally they can find great fulfilment from this attachment. Anuradha fulfil Uttara Phalguni's need for pure love. Together they can transcend any kind of obstacle or opposition. Rohini and Mrigasira also make very good partners for Uttara Phalguni.

Least compatible: Uttara Phalguni's solar rulership means that they are compatible with most signs. They are full of such warmth and generosity that they are able to connect with most nakshatras on an above average level. Ashlesha's independence and Mula's spiritual conflicts may be difficult for them to handle, but they will try to work at relationships with these nakshatras.

Ideal sexual partner: Uttara Phalguni, the Bull, connects well with the cow, Uttara Bhadra. Uttara Bhadra know how to satisfy the deepest desires of Uttara Phalguni. They are very compatible in other areas of life as well, making this a happy, long-lasting and completely contented relationship.

Unsuitable sexual partners: The worst sexual partners for Uttara Phalguni are the tigers, Chitra and Vishakha. Bulls have a practical approach to both life and sexuality, while Chitra and Vishakha yearn for the exotic. Uttara Phalguni find them too superficial, and Chitra and Vishakha find Uttara Phalguni unimaginative.
For complete relationship information see pages 128–139.

CUSPS

Those born at the end or beginning of the Uttara Phalguni should check the cusp details on page 141.

Hasta

26 SEPTEMBER TO 10 OCTOBER

Key Words: Yoga and individuality

Ruled by: The Moon	
Symbol: Palm of the hand	
Animal sign: Buffalo	
Deity: Savitar, the Sun god	
Motivation: Moksha	
Guna triplicity: Tamas, Tamas and Rajas	
Ayurvedic dosha: Vata	
Colour: Green	
Best direction: South	
Special consonants for birth names: Pu, Sha, Naa, Tha	
Principal stars: Al-Auwa.	
Western signs: Libra	

Meaning and Mythology

Hasta is placed entirely in the sign of Libra, which is ruled by Venus. The ruler of Hasta is the Moon. The Moon controls the mind and Venus gives inspiration and intuition. This nakshatra is connected to the mind and its ability to establish relationships with the universal energy that binds all forms of existence.

'Hasta' means 'the hand'. The hand reflects the destiny of a person and represents individual effort. Hasta develops potential through self-effort and understanding the laws of nature. The Moon waxes and wanes, and its rulership of this nakshatra therefore makes for changing perspectives and moving realities. Hasta learns through these experiences and works with the higher intellect of Venus. Venus is also known as Brighu, the great guru who laid down the Dharma Shastra or the right social and spiritual behaviour. Venus is rooted in spirituality, but its main form of action is in the material world. Libra provides the balance between material and spiritual. Hasta gives the individual the ability to change and grow in different directions.

The most famous Hasta was Mahatma Gandhi who, through religious belief and non-violent action, changed the direction of humanity.

Symbol
HAND

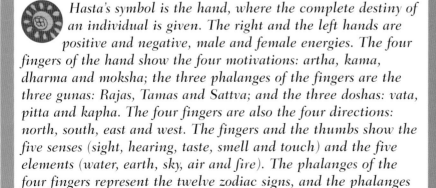

Hasta's symbol is the hand, where the complete destiny of an individual is given. The right and the left hands are positive and negative, male and female energies. The four fingers of the hand show the four motivations: artha, kama, dharma and moksha; the three phalanges of the fingers are the three gunas: Rajas, Tamas and Sattva; and the three doshas: vata, pitta and kapha. The four fingers are also the four directions: north, south, east and west. The fingers and the thumbs show the five senses (sight, hearing, taste, smell and touch) and the five elements (water, earth, sky, air and fire). The phalanges of the four fingers represent the twelve zodiac signs, and the phalanges of the thumbs and fingers are the 30 days of the solar month.

Ruling deities

The ruling deity of Hasta is Savitar, one of the 12 sons of Aditi. The 12 sons of Aditi symbolize the 12 signs of the zodiac from Aries to Pisces. Aditi represents infinity and her sons are different expressions of this eternal energy.

Savitar is connected to yoga. The practice of yoga helps us to control the mind and body and allows us to recognize our Inner Light. Savitar is also connected to the Gayatri Mantra.

HASTA AIM IS FOR MOKSHA

Hasta crave Moksha, the highest degree of perfection, but their outward karma is in the material field. Hasta realize that in pursuit of spiritual enlightenment, they need to harness their energies. They may turn to yoga, which will teach them to balance their physical life with their spiritual direction. There may be conflict to begin with as Hasta learn the lessons of letting go, but they can achieve peace and harmony.

GUNAS TRIPLICITY: TAMAS, TAMAS AND RAJAS

The psychological quality of Hasta is Tamas on the primary (physical) and secondary (mental) levels and Rajas on the tertiary (spiritual) level. The guna of Tamas is about intense involvement in the material process of life. The conflict arises from Rajas on the tertiary level, which does not allow Hasta to be completely happy with its material involvement. Hasta are engrossed in their desires, but on a spiritual level Rajas forces them to look beyond the material realities of today.

AYURVEDIC DOSHA IS VATA

Hasta is vata, reflecting the natural qualities of action, agility, and conflict. Hasta people often suffer from nervousness beneath their calm exteriors and are always trying to control their anxieties. This can stress them out very quickly. Hasta have to learn to stay calm. Yoga, or any kind of physical discipline that addresses both the mind and the body, will be good for Hasta. They need to express their vata energy.

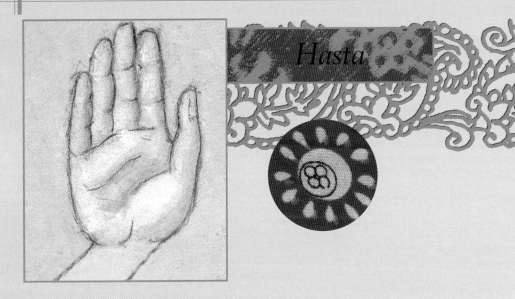

Hasta

CHARACTERISTICS/ PERSONALITY TRAITS

Hasta are generally charming, interesting and beautiful. They can appear materialistic on the surface. Beneath their exterior, however, they may be restless and unhappy with their material successes. They are searching for something more spiritual.

They can be very moody. The Moon rules this nakshatra and they will reflect all the waxing and waning phases of their ruler. Their moods annoy them; they will try to control and understand this side of their nature. Hasta should recognize the rhythms of the lunar cycle and learn to relate to them.

Hasta are considered lucky. Hard work and individual responsibility are part of their nature; they will do whatever is required to achieve their ambitions. They feel they are responsible for making their own destinies. While they are involved in the struggle to achieve success, they often experience sudden openings or good fortune, which reward their efforts well beyond expectations.

HOW IT LINKS WITH THE WESTERN SUN SIGN AND RULER

Hasta in Libra: Libra balances the opposing forces of negative and positive. Under Libra, Hasta learn stillness on a physical level, but the mind, represented by Hasta's ruler the Moon, is active and constantly searching. For Hasta to find true happiness they must learn to achieve peace of mind, by finding the right balance between their opposing desires.

SPIRITUAL LIFE PATH

Hasta represent the dawn of spiritual consciousness. Their spiritual path is connected to this realization. Although they may appear to be content leading mundane and ordinary lives, deep inside they may feel empty and incomplete. As consciousness of the higher truths dawns on them, the void will start to fill. The true path for Hasta is to realize this new reality and work towards it, while also being true to their earthly responsibilities.

RELATIONSHIPS

Hasta will have many and varied relationships. They may appear selfish, yet they can be the most generous of people. Partners of Hasta may feel they are more loving to other people. They can be practical about their relationships. They will give a lot materially, but emotionally they still feel unsettled. They can be extremely moody and need a lot of emotional support. While they appear confident and in control of their life, their inner self is often feeling vulnerable and restless. Although Hasta can feel trapped within a relationship, once they are truly committed they will usually be caring and giving.

SEXUAL ENERGY LINKED TO THE FEMALE BUFFALO

Buffaloes are wild animals who live near swamps and jungles; but they are also domesticated – in India they plough fields and give milk. Both the above factors are reflected in Hasta sexuality. They need independence and have a wild, untamed side to their nature. They can also be very sensuous and earthy. On the negative side, they can be aggressive and crude, although they usually keep this side of their nature controlled.

FAMOUS HASTA

Mahatma Gandhi, Brigitte Bardot, Gore Vidal, Julie Andrews, Susan Sarandon.

HOW HASTA RELATES TO OTHER NAKSHATRAS

Most compatible: Hasta enjoy the best relationship with Mrigasira. Hasta love Mrigasira for their intellectual power, and they can help Mrigasira to get in touch with their softer emotional side. Chitra understand Hasta's vulnerabilities; they support them emotionally, but their sexual compatibility is not strong so they must work on bettering it. Hasta enjoy relationships with Purva Ashadha; both are changeable and seek excitement from life. This relationship can baffle others. There does not seem to be any commitment to each other, yet they are able to survive the ups and downs of life.

Least compatible: The Moon rules Hasta, and nakshatras with lunar rulerships are usually able to have good relationships. Hasta will love others until they are disappointed or let down. They tend to see the best in others and this makes people show their better qualities. Ashwini and Shatabhishak are least compatible for Hasta; this is due to a complete lack of sexual compatibility.

Ideal sexual partner: Hasta, the female buffalo, finds sexual happiness with its male counterpart, Swati, who helps to release their sensual nature. Hasta usually keep their sexuality under wraps. With Swati there is no need for subterfuge as they instinctively connect to Hasta's true earthy nature.

Unsuitable sexual partners: Hasta are hostile to the horses, Ashwini and Shatabhishak. Hasta control their sexuality under a practical and pragmatic exterior, and Ashwini and Shatabhishak are unable to break through this barrier. *For complete relationship information see pages 128–139.*

CUSPS

Those born at the end or beginning of the Hasta should check the cusp details on page 141.

Chitra

10 OCTOBER TO 23 OCTOBER

Key Word: Beauty

Ruled by: Mars	
Symbol: Pearl	
Animal sign: Tiger	
Deity: Tvashtar, the celestial architect	
Motivation: Kama	
Guna triplicity: Tamas, Tamas and Tamas	
Ayurvedic dosha: Pitta	
Colour: Black	
Best direction: West	
Special consonants for birth names: Pay, Po, Raa, Ree	
Principal stars: Spica	
Western signs: Libra	

Meaning and Mythology

Chitra is placed in Libra, ruled by Venus. Mars rules Chitra. The combination of Mars and Venus brings out a passionate nature. Venus is the planet of love, romance, marriage and inspiration. Mars is the planet of action, leadership and courage. Under Chitra the process begins of unfolding the hidden nature of man.

'Chitra' means 'a reflection' or 'a beautiful picture', and Chitra reflects the potential of the soul. Chitra people are also usually very attractive.

Chitra have two types of life experience. On one hand they may be almost unaware of their spiritual potential, but on the other, circumstances and situations will force them to recognize their higher nature and reform their personality. The process is painful: the ego has to be cut away so that the inner soul can emerge.

Chitra represent new levels of achievement reached through personal life experiences. The old personality has to be completely re-fashioned to produce a new person who has an immense ability to influence those around them.

Symbol
THE PEARL

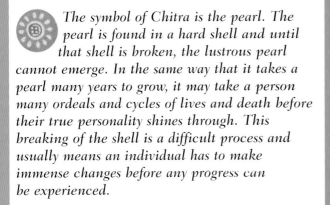

The symbol of Chitra is the pearl. The pearl is found in a hard shell and until that shell is broken, the lustrous pearl cannot emerge. In the same way that it takes a pearl many years to grow, it may take a person many ordeals and cycles of lives and death before their true personality shines through. This breaking of the shell is a difficult process and usually means an individual has to make immense changes before any progress can be experienced.

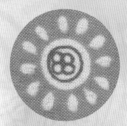

Ruling deities

Tvashtar, the ruling deity of Chitra, is the celestial architect. Symbolically, Tvashtar takes an uncut stone and turns it into a beautiful statue. The uncut stone is the human being encased in the world of matter. As Chitra are bound in Tamas, their true beauty is hidden, but as Tvashtar begins to cut away at the material life slowly their Inner Light starts to come through.

CHITRA AIM IS FOR KAMA

Kama is desires and needs on a very practical level. Chitra's passion is for expressing life to the fullest. They live life on two polarities: the intensely material and the completely spiritual. Chitra will express their passion equally in these two worlds.

GUNA TRIPLICITY: TAMAS, TAMAS AND TAMAS

The psychological quality of Chitra is completely bound in Tamas on all levels. Tamas keeps Chitra attached to their earthy desires. It becomes a crust keeping Chitra involved in their desires. The Tamas guna has been said to equate with ignorance, but its true quality encompasses the worldly life. When gunas crystallize together, there can also be a great breakthrough towards liberation.

AYURVEDIC DOSHA IS PITTA

Chitra are leaders: they are dynamic and full of energy. Chitra are ambitious and driven to make a mark in society. They are generous, creative, knowledgeable and intelligent. They can also be passionate and sensuous. Chitra do not recognize their own fallibility and can be short-tempered. Chitra have the capacity to burn out if they do not pace themselves properly.

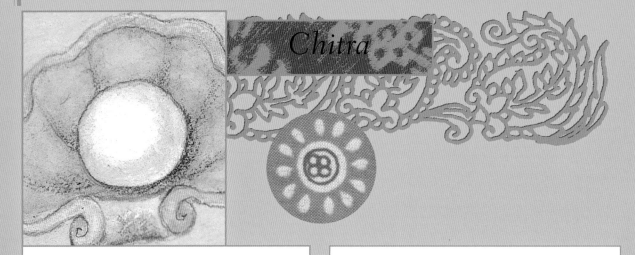

Chitra

CHARACTERISTICS/ PERSONALITY TRAITS

Chitra are attractive, charismatic, intelligent and natural leaders. They are sociable and are usually good at sports. They will often wear the most striking clothes and enjoy dressing in unusual fashions. When in public, they are fond of talking and seem to enjoy public events, but Chitra are in fact solitary by nature, they like their own space. They make acquaintances easily, but are wary of close friendships.

Chitra have many ideas and have the ability to turn these into reality. One should not reject their ideas out of hand, however outlandish they may seem. Their power of intuition allows them to see into the future and understand trends before their time.

On the negative side, Chitra can be fickle, constantly searching for excitement and becoming bored easily. They find it difficult to commit to any one thing, as there are always new ideas, hobbies, jobs and relationships to entice them.

Chitra are the dramatists of the zodiac. They like to live life on a grand scale. They are leaders and commanders: the world is their field of operation and they want to make an impact on it. They are not afraid of problems or setbacks in life. Dealing with obstacles tests their abilities, courage and stamina, and allows their strong personality to shine.

HOW IT LINKS WITH THE WESTERN SUN SIGN AND RULER

Chitra in Libra: Chitra is in the sign of Libra. It is exactly at the opposite point of Ashwini where the first soul comes into being. Libra represents the scales of justice, the true balance of life. Chitra learn to work for justice and peace. Chitra enjoy the fine things in life; they have a good eye for beauty in all forms. They are creative and much of their life is spent expressing their creativity. The creativity here is not in the physical form of children, but of ideas and inspiration. Chitra are often found in the world of the arts – as actors, writers, painters etc.

SPIRITUAL LIFE PATH

Chitra spirituality is connected to Sattva and moksha, but is involved in an essentially material world. The pearl, Chitra's symbol, is also called mukta. Mukta in Sanskrit is derived from mukti and moksha, both standing for spiritual enlightenment. Chitra focuses on this highest form of personal ambition while still being responsible for discharging its mundane responsibilities.

RELATIONSHIPS

Chitra often learn to be self-sufficient at a very young age. They want to share their life with someone, yet they are never able to give 100 per cent of themselves. Others often do not understand Chitra or their relationships. One of the reasons why Chitra relationships do not work is that they do not give them enough time. They will feel dissatisfied within themselves and restless to experience something new.

SEXUAL ENERGY LINKED TO THE FEMALE TIGER

Tiger sexuality is supposed to be the strongest in the animal kingdom. Chitra are virile and sensuous. They need partners who can match their strong sexuality. This is an area in which Chitra should never compromise. They are passionate, but their passion is the slow-burning type. They enjoy being wooed in comfortable and stylish surroundings. Chitra can be possessive and they may fight to establish their claim on a partner. However, if they decide to withdraw themselves from the sexual race, they can remain celibate and detached from others.

FAMOUS CHITRA

Luciano Pavarotti, Lily Langtry, Roger Moore, Oscar Wilde, Martina Navratilova.

HOW CHITRA RELATES TO OTHER NAKSHATRAS

Most compatible: Chitra's best relationship is with Hasta. Hasta's ability to love Chitra for what they are creates a powerful bond, which allows their relationship to survive and remain loving. With Mula, Chitra can create a wonderful partnership that is both exciting and loving. Vishakha answer Chitra's silent call for a deeply passionate partner who respects their independence and is not intimidated by their strong personality.

Least compatible: Purva Phalguni and Bharani are the worst relationships for Chitra. They are ruled by Venus, and Chitra is ruled by Mars. Mars/Venus relationships are largely based on sexual attraction, and there is not enough compatibility in other areas for a relationship to survive long term. Chitra feel uncomfortable with Anuradha's possessiveness as it is too restrictive.

Ideal sexual partner: Vishakha, the male tiger, is able to fulfil Chitra's every desire. The tigers are considered to have the strongest sexuality in the animal kingdom. Vishakha is the partner that understands Chitra's strong sexual drive, and is also interesting and intelligent.

Unsuitable sexual partners: The worst sexual partners for Chitra are the bull, Uttara Phalguni, and the cow, Uttara Bhadra. The tigers, Chitra and Vishakha, have the strongest sexual desires of all the nakshatras, and they must have a relationship that is sexually exciting. Uttara Phalguni and Uttara Bhadra are so diametrically opposite to Chitra that it may be better for them not to experiment with these relationships.

For complete relationship information see pages 128–139.

CUSPS

Those born at the end or beginning of the Chitra should check the cusp details on pages 141–2.

Swati

23 OCTOBER TO 6 NOVEMBER

Key Words: Success, ambition and dissatisfaction

Ruled by: Rahu	
Symbol: Coral	
Animal sign: Buffalo	
Deity: Vayu, the god of wind and life breath	
Motivation: Artha	
Guna triplicity: Tamas, Tamas and Sattva	
Ayurvedic dosha: Kapha	
Colour: Black	
Best direction: North	
Special consonants for birth names: Ru, Ray, Ra, Ta	
Principal stars: Arcturus	
Western signs: Libra (23 October) and Scorpio (24 October to 6 November)	

Symbol
CORAL

Swati's symbol is coral, which has a hard outer sheath and is self-propagating. It both affects and is affected by the marine environment it lives in. This symbolizes the human being; he lives in the world that influences his life, but in turn, he makes an impact on the world around him. Swati influence those around them; but they also use the influence of society to improve themselves.

Meaning and Mythology

The second nakshatra ruled by Rahu is Swati. The first day of Swati is in the sign of Libra, ruled by Venus, and the rest is in Scorpio, ruled by Mars. (Vedic astrology uses traditional rulerships and therefore does not recognize Pluto as the ruler of Scorpio.) Under Swati, the impulse is all about material gain. Venus rules the earthly needs in an individual while Mars provides the courage to go where no one has been before. Combining these with Rahu adds further to the desire for success, wealth and finance. Many millionaires are born in Swati; Bill Gates, the founder of Microsoft, being one of the most famous.

'Swati' means 'sword'. The sword can be used for both negative and positive purposes. Swati carries the sword as a tool for self-advancement, cutting through competition and obstacles in their path. Swati is also the name of one of the Sun's wives. In Swati, the Sun forgets its spiritual purpose and becomes entwined in the pleasures and pains of relationships. For a moment, it is not bothered about finding moksha or enlightenment.

The ruling deity is Vayu, which is the Prana. Pranayama or the control of Prana forms the basis of yoga. When individuals learn to harness the forces within them, they are able to control life. The yogis believe that we are going to live a certain number of breaths rather than a number of years. The mastery of this breath gives the yogis the ability to control the duration of their lives. Prana disciplines the mind; practice of pranayama gives the ability to control the wavering mind.

Ruling deities

The ruling deity, Vayu (atmosphere), rules the material world along with Agni (Fire) and Surya (the Sun). Vayu controls the intellect. Vayu is the Prana, the breath or the life force within human beings that connect them to the eternal energy. Pranayama or control of Prana forms the basis of yoga. When an individual learns to harness the life force they are able to control their lives.

SWATI AIM IS FOR ARTHA

Swati are motivated by artha, which is activity on a material plain. Swati are materialistic and will take practical steps to make their dreams come true. They are concerned with achieving success in this world. Artha is important if they are to achieve their ambitions.

GUNA TRIPLICITY: TAMAS, TAMAS AND SATTVA

The psychological quality of Swati is Tamas on the primary (physical) and secondary (mental) levels. Tamas keeps them bound to their earthly desires.

Fulfilment of tamasic desires creates a cycle of fulfilment and dissatisfaction. The subtle impulse of Sattva on the tertiary (spiritual) level gives Swati an idealistic self. Their inner purity is at odds with the materialistic way they live their life.

AYURVEDIC DOSHA IS KAPHA

Swati's kapha nature makes them calm and philosophical. Swati can be very placid in the competitive world. This makes them good industrialists and business people; they will remain calm whatever the crisis.

Swati

CHARACTERISTICS/ PERSONALITY TRAITS

Swati are always on the go. There is so much to do and achieve that Swati find themselves unable to decide which ambition they should fulfil next. Swati are 'ideas' people; they are disciplined and have the ability to turn their ideas into profitable realities. Many of their ideas are new or undiscovered. Rahu, their ruler, gives them the ability to take risks that others would avoid.

Swati are good strategists and may become involved in politics. They know how to plan, manoeuvre and play power games. However, their motivation is idealistic, as revealed by their inner quality of Sattva, and they can never understand when others accuse them of being underhand or manipulative.

Swati want to make an impact on their environment. They are focused, ambitious and practical. They have the ability to build wealth and they want to be rich. Their only problem occurs when they do not recognize their own limitations. This can result in loss of money, status and respect. Swati need to be the best – they set great store by achievements. However, their achievements do not always bring them the happiness they desired. This leads them to create higher and higher targets for themselves. When you meet Swati, you may feel confused by their hunger for success despite the fact that they appear to have achieved their life's ambitions.

HOW IT LINKS WITH THE WESTERN SUN SIGN AND RULER

Swati in Libra: Being born at the very end of Libra and the beginning of Swati (23 October) is a karmic birth time. Swati have immense wisdom and power to pursue their ambitions, materially and spiritually.

Swati in Scorpio: Rahu has ambitious ideas and Mars provides the physical capacity to fulfil them. But they are two polarities and there is not the balance of Libra. Swati/Scorpio will find they are pulled in different directions, which creates stress and tension in their lives.

SPIRITUAL LIFE PATH

Swati's life path is concerned with making a name in the world. They need to be practical: creating wealth and successful businesses are part of their spiritual make-up. They must not feel inadequate if they are to express their spirituality fully. Their spiritual path will take on its higher purpose when they learn to understand their life force or prana, and begin to harness this energy through yoga and meditation.

RELATIONSHIPS
Swati is the name of one of the Sun's wives. Marriage and committed relationships are an important part of Swati's agenda. Swati will search for an ideal partner but they can take their idealism too far. The perfection they demand from their partners may not be realistic. They can become dissatisfied with their relationships, and can be critical and fault-finding. This can spoil a good relationship and create unhappiness for them.

SEXUAL ENERGY LINKED TO THE MALE BUFFALO
Buffaloes are wild animals who live near swamps and jungles, but they are also domesticated – in India they are used to plough the fields.

Swati can be extremely sensuous and earthy. However, they may keep this side of their nature concealed, only expressing it to those very close to them. Sex usually takes a back seat to other ambitions. Swati do not place too much emphasis on their sexuality. They also have the ability to control their ardour. They can wait for the right time to satisfy their desires.

FAMOUS SWATI
Bill Gates, Pablo Picasso, Dylan Thomas, Marie Antoinette, Vivien Leigh.

HOW SWATI RELATES TO OTHER NAKSHATRAS
Most compatible: Swati find best compatibility with Bharani, who give them true companionship and love. Swati also work well with Ashwini, Ardra, Punarvasu, Hasta, other Swati and Purva Ashadha. With Ashwini, there will be few sexual sparks, so they will have to work extra hard to keep passion alive.

Least compatible: Swati try to make even the most difficult relationships work for them. Their most difficult task comes with Revati. Revati are only interested in spiritual life; they seek a partner who can give them spiritual fulfilment. Swati are practical and involved in the mundane pursuits of life. Each finds it difficult to understand the other and unless they are both extremely tolerant of each other's ambitions, this relationship is sure to become trenchant and frustrating.

Ideal sexual partner: Swati, the male buffalo, finds sexual happiness with its female mate, Hasta. Swati hide their sexual needs, usually expressing themselves in other ways. Hasta connects to Swati's sexual desires and together they find a fulfilment that is not possible with other nakshatras.

Unsuitable sexual partners: Swati find the sexuality of the horses, Ashwini and Shatabhishak, most difficult to handle. Swati enjoy sex as part of a committed relationship, but Ashwini and Shatabhishak are not always able to offer that. Horses are more spirited and highly strung, and they find it hard to reconcile themselves to the buffalo's pragmatism. *For complete relationship information see pages 128–139.*

CUSPS
Those born at the end or beginning of the Swati should check the cusp details on page 142.

Vishakha

6 NOVEMBER TO 19 NOVEMBER

Key Word: Wisdom and aspiration

Ruled by: Jupiter

Symbol: Potter's wheel

Animal sign: Male tiger

Deity: Agni, the god of fire, and Indra, the god of gods

Motivation: Dharma

Guna triplicity: Tamas, Sattva and Rajas

Ayurvedic dosha: Kapha

Colour: Gold

Best direction: East

Special consonants for birth names:
Te, Tu, Tay, To

Principal stars: Az-Zubanan, the two claws of Scorpio

Western signs: Scorpio

Symbol
POTTER'S WHEEL

The symbol of the potter's wheel shows the static inner core which is steeped in the Tamas of worldly illusions. The clay fashioned by the potter is likened to life, which is shaped in different ways by the hands of destiny; the experiences of life help it to mature.

Meaning and Mythology

Vishakha is placed entirely in the sign of Scorpio, ruled by Mars. Jupiter rules Vishakha.

'Vi' means 'to separate' and 'shakha' means 'a school'. The separation suggested in Vishakha is from materialism. 'Visha' means 'to enter' and 'Kha' means 'the heaven'. Vishakha stands for transformation and the aspiration to enter the heavens to connect with the eternal self.

Jupiter guides Vishakha through a stage where the soul is willing and able to take on board lessons and change its outlook. This change does not take place without great churning of emotions.

Jupiter and Mars are friends. Mars expresses his power on an earthly realm; here Jupiter teaches him to use his courage and inherent strength to move towards his spiritual self. Jupiter is benefic; it opposes conflict and believes in peace. Jupiter arranges favourable conditions so that the Martian impulses move towards spiritual growth. Scorpio creates the desire to unveil the original soul.

Vishakha are standing at the threshold of a new life. The change is yet to take place, as the soul is looking from outward to within. It has reached that point in life where there is a strong desire to go towards the inner sanctum, the great unknown. This can throw out negative and positive issues. There is no guarantee of the experience that awaits once inside.

Ruling deities

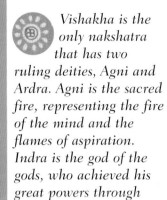

Vishakha is the only nakshatra that has two ruling deities, Agni and Ardra. Agni is the sacred fire, representing the fire of the mind and the flames of aspiration. Indra is the god of the gods, who achieved his great powers through meditation and self-sacrifice. Vishakha are at a junction of life where Agni burns away the superfluous and then Indra gives the capability to change the course of their life.

VISHAKHA AIM IS FOR DHARMA

Dharma motivates Vishakha, so doing the right thing is important to Vishakha. They face up to their responsibilities, socially and spiritually. They are keen to do their duty, and at times they will go beyond the call of duty. Vishakha can be dogmatic about their views.

GUNA TRIPLICITY: TAMAS, SATTVA AND RAJAS

The psychological quality of Vishakha is Tamas on a primary (physical) level, Sattva on the secondary (mental) level and Rajas on the tertiary (spiritual) level. All three gunas are reflected, showing a time of immense spiritual changes. Tamas indicates a life led on a practical level, the Sattvic mind is calm and pure, and Rajas shows that the real search is on a spiritual level.

AYURVEDIC DOSHA IS KAPHA

Vishakha are calm and patient even when life can be full of turmoil. So much is changing around them, but their kapha nature helps them to deal with it.

Vishakha

CHARACTERISTICS/ PERSONALITY TRAITS

Vishakha have two distinct personalities, which can cause them inner turmoil and grief. They are forever trying to reconcile the complicated needs of their two egos. They usually appear to be pleasure-loving people with larger-than-life personalities. Vishakha have many admirers and friends and are always surrounded by people whom they are advising, guiding and nurturing.

They are ambitious and aim for success, but material success does not always satisfy them. Vishakha need to change their perspective of reality in order to feel fulfilled and happy. Vishakha have the natural ability to connect to people at various levels and have wide-ranging interests. They could as easily take up carpentry as a hobby as pursue interests in the occult. Vishakha are interested in unravelling the deep mysteries of nature. They should definitely try yoga, as their nakshatra is closely connected with it.

Vishakha have a good eye for clothes and are interested in fashion. They will wear the most striking clothes, although not necessarily the brightest.

They welcome obstacles so that they can show their true mettle. They will stay calm in crises. They are good people to seek advice from in difficult times. They will give their wisdom freely and have the ability to see the larger picture, which can be very helpful.

Vishakha like to drink and this can be one of their weaknesses.

HOW IT LINKS WITH THE WESTERN SUN SIGN AND RULER

Vishakha in Scorpio: Scorpio represents hidden power which when properly harnessed can give tremendous ability. Jupiter bestows knowledge and wisdom. Vishakha stands for transformation. Vishakha/Scorpio energy has immense capabilities. They can use their powers to achieve full expression, spiritually and materially, or they can use it wastefully and debilitate themselves.

SPIRITUAL LIFE PATH

Vishakha's spiritual life path is concerned with facing up to change. This is an important nakshatra connected to transformation. Vishakha's spiritual path is about understanding the two polarities of life. They have to learn detachment while still being involved in material life. This is a time of preparation, not necessarily of total change. Vishakha need to look within themselves and discover their own power, rather than looking at the outside world to provide the answers.

RELATIONSHIPS

Vishakha can be very involved in relationships, yet remain detached. The restlessness they feel in their personal life can create immense dissatisfaction within themselves and can lead them to change partners constantly or to be untrue to their current ones. They need to look within themselves for answers and learn to understand their restlessness. Unless they do this, they may cause themselves great unhappiness. This is one of the reasons why Vishakha may have unsettled relationships early on in life. With age comes wisdom and the ability to deal with their restlessness.

SEXUAL ENERGY LINKED TO THE MALE TIGER

Vishakha are virile and potent. They have strong sexual appetites and will hunt out partners who can match this. If their partners cannot match their sexual needs, Vishakha must look elsewhere and never compromise, as this can lead to deep unhappiness.

Vishakha struggle with their intense sexuality; they may learn to conquer it and move towards celibacy and temperance. However, their sexuality is always smouldering below the surface and, given the right conditions, it can instantly return to its full force.

FAMOUS VISHAKHA

Hillary Clinton, Marie Curie, Katharine Hepburn, Auguste Rodin, Robert Louis Stevenson.

HOW VISHAKHA RELATES TO OTHER NAKSHATRAS

Most compatible: Vishakha are extremely restless and this creates problems for them in making commitments. As Chitra understand this restlessness and have a deep understanding of their sexual and emotional needs, they make the best partners for Vishakha. Jyeshta have the ability to keep the fickle Vishakha interested and this keeps their passions alive and burning.

Least compatible: Revati is the worst partner for Vishakha. Revati have reached an advanced stage of spiritual development and have little interest in the material world, while Vishakha need a strongly sensuous partner. At the first hint of trouble, they can become intolerant of each other's outlook. Revati will immediately express their disappointment in Vishakha and Vishakha will quickly move on to new pastures. For this relationship to survive, they have to learn how to work through the difficult periods.

Ideal sexual partner: Chitra, the female tiger, is the best partner for the male tiger, Vishakha. With Chitra, there can be a sizzling relationship that is full of sensuous pleasure and sexuality. Tigers are considered to have the strongest sexuality in the animal kingdom. Chitra fulfil Vishakha's needs completely.

Unsuitable sexual partners: The worst sexual partners for Vishakha are the bull, Uttara Phalguni, and the cow, Uttara Bhadra. Uttara Phalguni and Uttara Bhadra are too practical and earthy to fulfil the exotic desires of Vishakha. *For complete relationship information see pages 128–139.*

CUSPS

Those born at the end or beginning of the Vishakha should check the cusp details on page 142.

Anuradha

19 NOVEMBER TO 2 DECEMBER

Key Words: Divine love

Ruled by: Saturn	
Symbol: Lotus	
Animal sign: Female deer	
Deity: Mitra, the god of light	
Motivation: Dharma	
Guna triplicity: Tamas, Sattva and Tamas	
Ayurvedic dosha: Pitta	
Colour: Red brown	
Best direction: South	
Special consonants for birth names: Na, Nee, Nu, Nay	
Principal stars: Three stars at the head of Scorpionis	
Western signs: Scorpio (19 to 22 November) and Sagittarius (23 November to 2 December)	

Meaning and Mythology

Anuradha is placed partly in Scorpio, ruled by Mars, and partly in Sagittarius, ruled by Jupiter. Saturn rules Anuradha. The portion of Anuradha ruled by Mars gives us the courage and confidence to face the spiritual trials and tribulations that Saturn puts in our path. The latter half, ruled by Jupiter, provides the balance to saturnine restrictions.

'Anuradha' has several meanings. It means 'a small flash of lightning' or 'a tiny spark', suggesting that it takes only a small flash of intuition or a tiny spark of consciousness to make us aware of our connection with the divine. 'Anu' also means small and 'Radha' is the name of the beloved of Lord Krishna. Radha was a separate entity to Krishna, but desired to merge with him. Again, the meaning of Anuradha is connecting the individual to the entirety of the universe.

The soul immersed in the material world forgets its divine heritage. Anuradha unveils its hidden purity. Anuradha opens our minds to the Kundalini, the mysterious power within us, which we need to activate to reach the path of higher consciousness. As we start to understand and access the hidden power within us we must be careful. The knowledge of our secret faculties has to be handled carefully as it can create turmoil within our normal life.

Symbol
LOTUS

The symbol of Anuradha is the lotus, which flourishes in stagnant waters. The lotus casts its seeds in the mud and the flowers grow towards the solar energy. Once it has flowered, it withers away and returns to the mud, where it will root again to repeat the whole process. The lotus is said to flower so that it can be laid at the feet of the gods, the soul is born to experience life and death so that it can break away from the cycle to find enlightenment.

Ruling deities

Mitra, the ruling deity of Anuradha, is a personification of the Sun. Mitra is one of the 12 sons of Aditi, the universal mother. Mitra rules daylight. It unveils the experiences of the night, the time spent by an individual in harnessing their power. In Anuradha, it exposes the latent potential that has become hidden by a life engulfed in materialism. Mitra helps to get rid of our darkness by giving us light.

ANURADHA AIM IS FOR DHARMA

Dharma motivates Anuradha. They recognize their duty to both the divine and the material worlds. Anuradha will be equally concerned about doing the right thing in the world they live in and expressing their dharmic tendencies in the search for higher truths. This can make them self-righteous at times, as if they are the only ones who have uncovered these new horizons.

GUNA TRIPLICITY: TAMAS, SATTVA AND TAMAS

The psychological quality of Anuradha is Tamas on a primary (physical) level, Sattva on the secondary (mental) level and Tamas on the tertiary (spiritual) level. Tamas' outer sheath reflects the life being led on a material level. The Sattvic mind indicates purity and truth. But Tamas on a spiritual level does not allow the purity to shine through. The Tamas/Sattva combination is of two opposites. Anuradha can feel torn by the two polarities of their life, until they understand how to connect them.

AYURVEDIC DOSHA IS PITTA

Anuradha are charitable, aesthetic, learned and bright. They can be hot-headed and short-tempered. They are energetic, forceful, charismatic and stimulating. They are leaders and innovators. Anuradha are ambitious: they will work hard to achieve their goals. Pitta people usually find it difficult to delegate and end up taking far too much responsibility.

Anuradha

CHARACTERISTICS/ PERSONALITY TRAITS

Anuradha's life and emotions are split into polarities. They can be spiritual yet extremely materialistic; kind yet cruel; sparkling company one minute and depressed the next. At times there is no happy medium. They are always trying to find a balance. In this search they can experience many up and downs, then suddenly the mist clears and when they become aware of how to deal with the conundrum of their life, they will be able to find success, happiness and peace.

Anuradha may feel weighed down by their responsibilities. They sometimes feel they carry the burden of the world on their shoulders. Their life is a never-ending search for excellence. Sometimes they live too much in the future and forget to enjoy the present. Anuradha should pay extra importance to their present life. The past has already happened; the future they have no control over. The present, if lived properly, will give them happiness and successes both in present and future lifetimes.

They are intelligent and active. Anuradha have experienced much in life and they have the ability to share this with others. They make wise counsellors and advisers.

Anuradha are good at projects that require endurance. Even boring jobs will not trouble Anuradha as long as they know there is a purpose behind all their hard work.

They are complex personalities. Not everyone can understand them, and people see many different sides to Anuradha. Some will see their bright and fun side, and others their serious and deep nature. As Anuradha find it difficult to understand themselves, it is even more difficult to unravel their personalities. Their personality develops gradually, and with time they will find peace and harmony.

HOW IT LINKS WITH THE WESTERN SUN SIGN AND RULER

Anuradha in Scorpio: Scorpio represents hidden power; Anuradha is the divine spark that can illuminate this power, but this creates problems. Mars wants to act while Saturn keeps bringing up karmic restrictions to allow the soul to mature enough to deal with this power.

Anuradha in Sagittarius: Sagittarius is the dawn of consciousness and Anuradha helps in this task. The path of Anuradha/Sagittarius is much easier: Jupiter provides wisdom to Saturn and balances its restrictive energy with its expansive one.

relationships. Anuradha's sexual relationships are coloured by their search for an ideal mate and this can make it hard for them to settle in one relationship.

HOW ANURADHA RELATES TO OTHER NAKSHATRAS

Most compatible: Anuradha's best partner is Jyeshta. With Jyeshta, they find harmony in every aspect of life: they are sexually fulfilled and emotionally connected, and their love is strong enough to face and survive the obstacles of life. Rohini answers Anuradha's silent need for love and together they can form an ideal partnership. Uttara Phalguni connects deeply with Anuradha. Their love is intense and any commitment they make will be able to withstand adversity and disagreements.

Least compatible: Anuradha is another nakshatra that tries to make relationships work with other nakshatras. Their most difficult partnership will be with Chitra, who can be uncaring and trample their fragile emotions. Chitra find Anuradha's love too restricting and Anuradha become jealous of Chitra's independence.

Ideal sexual partner: The male deer, Jyeshta, is the best sexual partner for the female deer, Anuradha. Jyeshta know how to woo Anuradha with love, as pure sexual compatibility will never be enough.

Unsuitable sexual partners: The dogs, Ardra and Mula, are the worst sexual partners for Anuradha. The practical dog can be insensitive to Anuradha's need to be wooed with words of love. Anuradha usually enjoy sex only if they feel their partner truly loves them; sexual relationships alone are not enough.
For complete relationship information see pages 128–139.

CUSPS
Those born at the end or beginning of the Anuradha should check the cusp details on page 142.

SPIRITUAL LIFE PATH
Anuradha's spiritual life path is being connected to the earthly pursuits while aspiring towards the divine. They must relate to a tree that has its roots firmly in the ground, but its branches spread towards the sky. Their aspiration to merge with the universal consciousness, to find their hidden soul, gives them immense ability to face life's difficulties.

RELATIONSHIPS
Anuradha's name is connected to Radha, the consort of Krishna. Krishna is considered the god of love and Radha aspired to be merged as one with him. Theirs was a divine love. Anuradha also seek this kind of true and idealistic love. More than any other nakshatra, Anuradha need love. They will be prepared to give up everything – family, country and wealth – for this love.

SEXUAL ENERGY LINKED TO THE FEMALE DEER
The deer is also considered to be another name for the Moon (see Mrigasira). The Moon loves passionately and emotionally, and so does the deer. Anuradha will not be involved in purely sexual relationships; they need sex that includes love. As the deer shed their antlers periodically, so Anuradha need to change

FAMOUS ANURADHA
Indira Gandhi, Goldie Hawn, Jimi Hendrix, Henri Toulouse-Lautrec, Charles Schultz.

Jyeshta

2 DECEMBER TO 15 DECEMBER

Key Word: Kundalini

Ruled by: Mercury	
Symbol: Earring	
Animal sign: Male deer	
Deity: Indra, the god of gods	
Motivation: Artha	
Guna triplicity: Tamas, Sattva and Sattva	
Ayurvedic dosha: Vata	
Colour: Cream	
Best direction: West	
Special consonants for birth names: No, Ya, and Ye, Yo	
Principal stars: Antares	
Western signs: Sagittarius	

Meaning and Mythology

Jyeshta is placed entirely in the sign of Sagittarius, ruled by Jupiter. Sagittarius is the herald of a new way based on a fresh perception of the meaning of life. Under this extremely powerful nakshatra, the soul breaks away from its materialistic course of life and moves towards the final part of its spiritual journey. This is not an easy task. The ruler of Jyeshta is Mercury, the celestial link between materialism and spiritualism. At Jyeshta the changes start, but if the soul is not ready, it struggles against the restrictions and this creates unhappiness.

'Jyeshta' means 'elder sister', 'the middle finger', or 'the holy river Ganges'. Thus it has esteem attached to it. In India the elder sister is looked upon with great respect as she is like one's mother. The river Ganges is said to wash away all our negative karma. The middle finger is the finger of destiny. It is used in yoga during pranayama to control the flow of breath. Pranayama is performed so that we are able to activate the Kundalini and the seven chakras. At Jyeshta, guidance is given to activate the Kundalini.

Jyeshta learn to control their 4senses with the practice of yoga. Yoga gradually unfolds the consciousness and unites the spiritual with the physical.

Symbol
EARRING

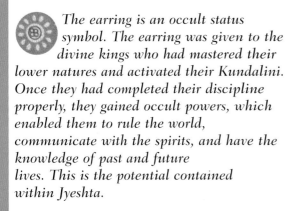

The earring is an occult status symbol. The earring was given to the divine kings who had mastered their lower natures and activated their Kundalini. Once they had completed their discipline properly, they gained occult powers, which enabled them to rule the world, communicate with the spirits, and have the knowledge of past and future lives. This is the potential contained within Jyeshta.

Ruling deities

Indra, the ruling deity, is considered the god of gods. Indra has the power to control our senses or 'indirayas'. He achieved this power after hard toil, penance and difficult lessons. He can enjoy the sensuality and pleasures of life, because he is privy to the secret of how to master them.

Indra is also considered to be the god of yoga.

JYESHTA AIM IS FOR ARTHA

Artha, the practical expression of life, motivates Jyeshta. They are still involved in achieving success on the material plane. Worldly success and status are important to Jyeshta. By gaining high esteem they will be able to pursue their spiritual interests. Jyeshta enjoy a luxurious life, and therefore they work hard and have practical goals to achieve it.

GUNA TRIPLICITY: TAMAS, SATTVA AND SATTVA

The psychological quality of Jyeshta is Tamas on a primary (physical) level, and Sattva on the secondary (mental) and tertiary (spiritual) levels. Jyeshta are involved in the world of matter, but their inner self is pure. The Tamas/ Sattva combination is a difficult one. Jyeshta can go from extreme materialism to pure idealism. Their life is usually divided into two halves: the first is strongly connected with material ambitions, but in the second, their inner soul forces them to follow a path of spiritual growth and personal chastity.

AYURVEDIC DOSHA IS VATA

Jyeshta reflect the natural qualities of vata. They are active and always on the go, tending to live on their nervous energies. They can experience allergies and breathing problems and can get stressed easily. Jyeshta need plenty of nourishing food and comfortable surroundings. They may appear to be self-assured and calm on the surface, but underneath they are a mass of nerves.

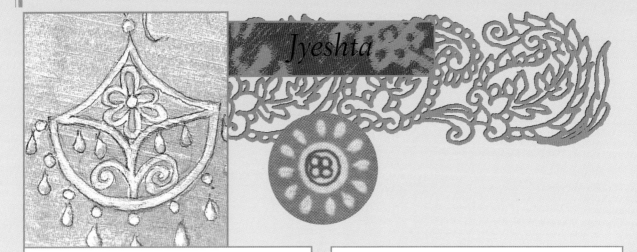

Jyeshta

CHARACTERISTICS/ PERSONALITY TRAITS

Jyeshta are in a position where they know life has to change. Whatever their given circumstances, they will feel the need to make important differences.

This nakshatra has a deep interest in the occult and the mysteries of the world, and they may have occult powers that they are not fully prepared to deal with. On one level they are greatly empowered to make changes as they know what others may not be aware of. In fact, Jyeshta are able to accomplish just about anything they put their minds to. If they set out to achieve something, they will be willing to face a lot of difficulties to get what they want.

Jyeshta represent the struggle of the mind. They are extremely bright and can be intellectual giants, but they feel their intellect can limit their perception and want to widen their scope. Jyeshta need to be careful with the techniques they employ to go beyond, and should avoid dabbling with the darker forces of nature. They are ambitious and want to achieve what others have not.

There are two distinct types of Jyeshta: one that expresses themselves on a purely material world and the other that connects with their spiritual side. They are usually successful in whatever they undertake. They have immense power and strength to reach their goals. If they experience any setbacks on their path, they will plan to overcome them.

Jyeshta are very disciplined. They like an ordered life. The only area where their discipline may not be strong is with drugs and alcohol, so they should take particular care around these substances which can create many problems for them.

HOW IT LINKS WITH THE WESTERN SUN SIGN AND RULER

Jyeshta in Sagittarius: Sagittarius brings with it a changed perception of reality and Jyeshta quickly understand this new reality. Jyeshta can transform difficulties into accomplishments, weakness into strength, and sexual love into spiritual love.

SPIRITUAL LIFE PATH

Jyeshta's life path is connected to yoga and pranayama. Once they bring these disciplines into their lives, they are able to realize their immense potential. They have to learn about the forces of their own nature. The material life is still important for Jyeshta, but they begin to understand the true power that rests within them. They stop searching in the outside world for the answers and start to look within themselves.

RELATIONSHIPS

Jyeshta can be highly sexed, sensual and possessive. They may get involved in bad relationships that can make them deeply unhappy. However, if they forge spiritual alliances with partners, their relationships can flourish beautifully.

Jyeshta are possessive, yet they also can be fickle. One moment they are madly in love; the next they have found someone else and have left their partner high and dry. Jyeshta like to be amused and titillated. They need partnerships that are intellectually stimulating.

SEXUAL ENERGY LINKED TO THE MALE DEER

Jyeshta are sexually active, and they find it difficult to commit to one person. Variety is the spice of life for them. Jyeshta like a deer are proud and beautiful. If they desire someone nothing will stand in their way. The deer can sometimes get into an intensely passionate state and if Jyeshta get too deeply involved, they may become obsessive and relentless in the pursuit of their sexual desires. In this state, they can be destructive to themselves and others.

FAMOUS JYESHTA

Maria Callas, Walt Disney, Frank Sinatra, Jane Austen, Gustave Eiffel.

HOW JYESHTA RELATES TO OTHER NAKSHATRAS

Most compatible: Anuradha and Magha are Jyeshta's best partners. With Anuradha, they find love that can withstand life's up and downs, creating happiness for them, sexually and emotionally. Magha's strength and independence appeal to Jyeshta, and they bring excitement and fun to each other's lives. Jyeshta want to be loved and Krittika make them feel secure. Wrapped in Krittika's warmth, Jyeshta's love flourishes.

Least compatible: Ardra and Punarvasu are the most difficult relationships for Jyeshta. Ardra are sexually incompatible, but there is also a constant fight for intellectual superiority. Jyeshta can be over-critical of Ardra and vice versa; this does little to create the right conditions for love to thrive. Jyeshta are unable to understand Punarvasu's need to love everyone. They want Punarvasu to love them alone, but when they realize that Punarvasu cannot love exclusively, Jyeshta will feel neglected and can become jealous and possessive.

Ideal sexual partner: Anuradha, the female deer, is the best sexual partner for Jyeshta. For Jyeshta, love and sexual happiness are entwined and Anuradha understand this. This makes their relationship deeply sensuous and loving.

Unsuitable sexual partners: The dogs, Ardra and Mula, are the worst sexual partners for Jyeshta. The pragmatic dogs do not understand Jyeshta's sexuality. Jyeshta will always feel incomplete in these relationships and therefore will satisfy their sensual needs elsewhere. *For complete relationship information, see pages 128–139.*

CUSPS

Those born at the end or beginning of the Jyeshta should check the cusp details on page 142.

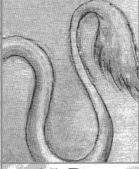

Mula

15 DECEMBER TO 28 DECEMBER

Key Words: The essence

Ruled by: Ketu	
Symbol: Tail of a lion or an elephant goad	
Animal sign: Male dog	
Deity: Niritti	
Motivation: Kama	
Guna triplicity: Sattva, Rajas and Rajas	
Ayurvedic dosha: Vata	
Colour: Mustard	
Best direction: North	
Special consonants for birth names: Yay, Yo, Ba, Be	
Principal stars: Vicrtau	
Western signs: Sagittarius (15 to 21 December) and Capricorn (22 to 28 December)	

Symbol
LION'S TAIL AND THE ELEPHANT GOAD

The elephant goad is used to guide the elephant in the correct direction. For people, this symbol represents the constant prodding or pain we have to suffer in our search for the spiritual pathway. The lion uses his tail to express his anger and supremacy. There can be immense anger directed at others. Power issues are also strong here. If the wisdom of Mula is not being expressed or channelled properly, it can lead to abuse of power.

Meaning and Mythology

Mula is the third nakshatra ruled by Ketu. It is placed partly in Sagittarius, ruled by Jupiter, and partly in Capricorn, ruled by Saturn. Mula is the start of the final part of the soul's mission towards finding the answers that will enable it to break away from the cycles of life and death. Ketu fulfils its role as a moksha planet by arousing the soul towards its ultimate destination. 'Mula' means 'root' and it is also muladhara chakra (the base chakra) which is the basis of spiritual growth.

Sagittarius transcends the physical into the psychic. The knowledge it contains has led the sages to equate the power of Sagittarius to the nine geniuses, nine planets, nine treasures of the god of wealth, nine emotions, nine poisons and nine creators. All this is reflected in the nine stars assigned to Sagittarius. Sagittarius is also the ninth sign of the zodiac; its ability to express itself on varied planes makes it an important changing point in life.

Capricorn provides the bridge between man and the Supreme, the higher forces. Qualities of renunciation and self-sacrifice are developed to activate the deeper levels of the soul. Now the individual is consciously cooperating with the divine plan.

Jupiter represents wisdom, Saturn renunciation, and Ketu is the past karma that we carry in the sub-conscious. All these combine to make Mula an intense nakshatra. Mula is rooted in earth, but it grows towards the sky and aspires to the universal connection.

Ruling deities

The deity that rules Mula is Niritti, the goddess of death and destruction. She personifies the destruction of the material sheath and the foundation on which spiritual enlightenment can be undertaken. The pain experienced by the influence of Mula changes the personality. This is the nakshatra of initiation towards spiritual realization.

MULA AIM IS FOR KAMA

Kama is passion – sexual, religious, for life, for a cause. At Mula, the passion may well be for sex, as this nakshatra is rooted in the desire. Once it learns to transcend these immediate needs, the passion can develop for spiritual development.

GUNA TRIPLICITY: SATTVA, RAJAS AND RAJAS

The psychological quality of Mula is Sattva on a primary (physical) level, and Rajas on the secondary (mental) and tertiary (spiritual) levels. This is the first time Sattva appears at the outer level of the individual. The change from Tamas to Sattva is a major change in psychological orientation. Although you are born in Mula, you will feel acutely the breaking of the Tamas and its links with materialism. In Mula the soul begins its journey on a completely new level of consciousness. Mula can be calm and spiritual on the outside but the Rajas within them creates major conflicts as they search for a new way of life.

AYURVEDIC DOSHA IS VATA

Mula reflect the natural qualities of vata. So much change has taken place in the psychology of Mula that they tend to live on their nerves. The new realities mean they have much to experience and understand. Their minds are greatly activated and they find it difficult to relax.

Mula

CHARACTERISTICS/ PERSONALITY TRAITS

Mula birth is where major changes take place. This has a great impact on the Mula personality. Whereas the other nakshatras have struggled with this new frontier, Mula adapts to it wholeheartedly. They learn to connect the physical, astral and mental bodies with the soul. They explore the secrets of nature, occult and psychic energy.

Mula are adventurous, brave and explore new frontiers. They are full of ideas and can make great leaders.

Mula are optimistic and cheerful. They will face adversity with equipoise. They can adapt to sudden changes in circumstances; this is part of their learning curve.

They tend to have a low boredom threshold. If life becomes too static, they will make changes. Sometimes they are responsible for creating their own insecurities, because they do not give themselves a chance to settle down.

Mula are disciplined and like to live an austere life. Usually, they will work towards creating a strong base for themselves. Even if they are extremely wealthy, they will enjoy living simply. Mula are the people who will voluntarily fast, go away to retreats and quietly live alone.

HOW IT LINKS WITH THE WESTERN SUN SIGN AND RULER

Mula in Sagittarius: As Mula/Sagittarius moves towards the path of self-discovery, the choices become increasingly harder. Conflict between the sexual and spiritual self emerges. This creates turbulence in their lives, as material achievements do not satisfy them, but their spiritual growth is still in infancy.

Mula in Capricorn: At Capricorn, man is still living in the practical world, but is moving towards his final path. In Capricorn/Mula, past karmas begin to activate, and many unexpected events happen to lessen the burden of this karma. Paying the price for past actions is not always an easy path.

SPIRITUAL LIFE PATH

It is important for Mula to remember that they are the root, so they are rooted in the physical, objective and the material. Nevertheless, their aspirations are for the spiritual and psychic. Their dissatisfaction with life will lessen once they realize that a tree needs strong roots to grow upwards. In the same way, Mula need to be practical and build up strong foundations in their life before they can move towards achieving their higher aspirations.

RELATIONSHIPS

Mula are indecisive and fickle in relationships: they can never make up their minds. This makes relationships difficult for them. Mula do not make responsible and stable partners. They can be exciting and changeable; they take pleasure in living life on the edge. They will be adventurous and enjoy an ever-changing landscape. Alternatively, they may decide to live a life of austerity and to live alone.

Mula find it difficult to confine themselves to traditional norms of behaviour in relationships. They are looking for an ideal that does not exist. They will experiment, change, and try to enjoy life to the full. They can be great companions. They can also have good long-term relationships providing their partners do not expect them to conform.

SEXUAL ENERGY LINKED TO THE MALE DOG

Mula are sexually connected to the male dog. They will actively pursue those that they love, and will be passionate and highly sexed. Mula have sensual personalities and they will have many sexual partners. This strong sexuality can worry them sometimes; it is a part of their nature they may want to change.

FAMOUS MULA

Uri Geller, Jane Fonda,
Mao Tse-Tung, Sir Isaac Newton,
Giacomo Puccini.

HOW MULA RELATES TO OTHER NAKSHATRAS

Most compatible: Purva Ashadha and other Mula are the best partners for Mula. Mula have unusual personalities, although they can be practical and make a commitment to the right person. They find Purva Ashadha fascinating and will stay with them through the changing phases of Purva Ashadha's life. Other Mula instinctively understand them and they can find happiness together. Mula are deeply attracted to Chitra, who love the contradictions of Mula's personality.

Least compatible: Mula tend to look beyond the purely illusionary nature of most relationships. Punarvasu bring out the worst in Mula. Mula will get annoyed by Punarvasu's manipulations; Punarvasu find Mula's personality difficult to handle and they can act out of character – Punarvasu usually find it easy to love others, but not Mula. The spiritual destinies of Mula and Uttara Phalguni are in conflict. Mula need to move towards the higher path and Uttara Phalguni feel that the higher path is to be found through material happiness.

Ideal sexual partner: Ardra, the female dog, is the best sexual partner for Mula. However, the overall relationship between Mula and Ardra is only average; Mula need more than just sexual compatibility in their true soulmate.

Unsuitable sexual partners: The deer, Jyeshta and Anuradha, do not relate to Mula sexually. Mula find them too idealistic about love and unrealistic about their sexual needs. Mula are pragmatic and stubborn; they will not be able to fulfil Jyeshta's sexual needs. *For complete relationship information, see pages 128–139.*

CUSPS

Those born at the end or beginning of Mula should check the cusp details on page 142.

Purva Ashadha

28 DECEMBER TO 11 JANUARY

Key Word: Charisma

Ruled by: Venus	
Symbol: Elephant's tusk	
Animal sign: Male monkey	
Deity: Apas, the water god	
Motivation: Moksha	
Guna triplicity: Sattva, Rajas and Tamas	
Ayurvedic dosha: Pitta	
Colour: Black	
Best direction: East	
Special consonants for birth names: Bu, Dha, Bha, Dhha	
Principal stars: An-Naaim	
Western signs: Capricorn	

Meaning and Mythology

The nakshatra of Purva Ashadha is in Capricorn. Saturn rules Capricorn and Venus rules Purva Ashadha. Saturn is the great teacher of cosmic truths. Venus is the spiritual teacher who advises humans. Purva Ashadha will lead us towards externalizing our inner strengths and finding our own light. There will be difficulties along the way, but Venus smoothes the path and creates situations where wisdom flourishes.

'Purva' means 'west' and 'Ashadha' means 'unsubdued'. It indicates what cannot be suppressed. The true nature of humans comes out regardless of what opposition they have to face. It is linked to the following nakshatra, Uttara Ashadha. Together they represent the common principle of unfolding new talents. In Purva Ashadha, there are still some blocks to expressing their nature fully, while Uttara Ashadha embraces the changes.

Purva Ashadha indicates discovery of new possibilities, externalization of latent faculties and the uncovering of one's most valuable qualities. The meaning of life can be suddenly revealed; hidden knowledge uncovered, intuitive faculties may be sharpened. Purva Ashadha develop knowledge and wisdom that can never be taken away from them.

Symbol
ELEPHANT'S TUSK

The symbol of the elephant's tusk shows the revelation of the inner faculties. The tusk is the most expensive part of the elephant. It is valued for its beauty and others will kill the elephant to try to own it. Others also value the knowledge that Purva Ashadha uncovers, but this can lead demonic forces to try to take away this new power. The tusk, if cut off, will grow again, showing that wisdom once gained cannot be taken away.

Ruling deities

Apas, the god of water, indicates the transforming nature of this nakshatra. Water is always used in rituals to cleanse and rejuvenate the inner soul. Water is purity and sattvic. Ganga Jal or the water of the river Ganges is used at all auspicious occasions. At Purva Ashadha the soul wants to cleanse its past sins to prepare itself for its final journey to understanding the purpose of life and finding fulfilment.

PURVA ASHADHA AIM IS FOR MOKSHA
Purva Ashadha are now moving towards moksha. They will voluntarily take this path. They understand the great responsibility resting on their shoulders. Purva Ashadha find enlightenment by using their own experiences to find their true potential.

GUNA TRIPLICITY: SATTVA, RAJAS AND TAMAS
The psychological quality of Purva Ashadha is the entwining of the three gunas. Tamas on the tertiary (spiritual) level indicates that something within them is blocking their path to pure expression. Rajas on the secondary

(mental) level keeps them searching for the philosophy, ideas or wisdom that will help them find themselves. Sattva on the primary (physical level) makes it clear their path is towards peace, purity and calmness. The inner conflict of gunas does not allow them to settle comfortably.

AYURVEDIC DOSHA IS PITTA
Purva Ashadha are active, forceful and charismatic. They are creative, intuitive and inspirational. They make good leaders, and are ambitious and hardworking. They are fiery in temperament. This fire quality is at odds with their Capricorn personality. Many creative people are born under this sign.

Purva Ashadha

CHARACTERISTICS/ PERSONALITY TRAITS

Purva Ashadha are creative, bright and intelligent. If they work with the talents they have been given, they can create wonderful and long-lasting results. Venus, their planetary ruler, gives them talent in the fields of art and entertainment. However successful they may be in their chosen career, they will always feel humble and self-effacing. Elvis Presley, the most famous Purva Ashadha, left behind a lasting and valuable legacy, yet he was never able to appreciate his own talent.

Purva Ashadha are changeable. They have the ability to re-invent themselves periodically – completely changing their ideas, personality and characteristics. They are like a salamander that changes colour. If they adapt a new philosophy of life, they will completely change their persona.

Purva Ashadha can be thought of as water, pure and clear to start with, but when mixed with any colour it will become that colour. They are constantly changing because they are taking in new ideas and developing. They are sometimes accused of being deceptive and not open about their true self. They are not deliberately trying to mislead anyone. At any given time they reflect the sum total of their personality, but because they take on board so much new information and adapt to new situations quickly, others may feel they have been deceived. One should never try to fully understand Purva Ashadha; they can be as clear as the water of a spring in the highest Himalayas, yet hide secrets within themselves that no one can fully decipher.

HOW IT LINKS WITH THE WESTERN SUN SIGN AND RULER

Purva Ashadha in Capricorn: Capricorn are practical, determined and disciplined; Purva Ashadha are fluid and capricious. Purva Ashadha must learn to recognize the contrary characteristics within their personality. They have strong creative urges and they need to be constantly on the move; if they can combine this with Saturn's responsibility and hard work, they will be well on the way to happiness.

SPIRITUAL LIFE PATH

Purva Ashadha's spiritual path is connected to understanding the final blocks that prevent their spiritual flowering. These can be relationships, career, family or friends. They have to learn how to deal with them and use the experiences of life to unravel their inner selves.

RELATIONSHIPS

Purva Ashadha are in a perpetual state of flux and this can make them difficult partners. Their personalities are constantly developing and changing. Anyone involved with a Purva Ashadha should know what to expect. They can be deeply involved with a partner, but may decide to adopt a completely new philosophy of life. If their partners are not willing to change with them, they will be left behind. Purva Ashadha can never stay in a boring relationship; they need to experience new situations and sensations. This may create difficulty with partners, if they are not able to articulate their inner needs.

SEXUAL ENERGY LINKED TO THE MALE MONKEY

Purva Ashadha are serial monogamists. When they vow to be true to a partner for ever, they mean it. But as their personality unfolds, their sexual needs change and they need to move on. If their partners can accept and understand their fluid personality, they may be able to stay together. Purva Ashadha are sexually creative and inspirational lovers; they have strong appetites and are always ready to make love. Their inner souls desire to experience life to the full.

FAMOUS PURVA ASHADHA

Elvis Presley, David Bowie, Mary Tyler Moore, Joan of Arc, J. R. R. Tolkien.

HOW PURVA ASHADHA RELATES TO OTHER NAKSHATRAS

Most compatible: Revati is the best partner for Purva Ashadha. Revati are able to deal with the changing nature of Purva Ashadha's ideals, and can change their personalities to fit in with them. Mula will give practical support to Purva Ashadha's ideas. Other Purva Ashadha also make good partners, but this relationship will always be redefining itself. Purva Ashadhas understand each other and stay committed throughout the continual changes in their lives.

Least compatible: Purva Ashadha are very adaptable and they find it easy to relate to others. It is commitment that can be a problem. Dhanishta is their most difficult partner. There is great initial passion, but after that has gone, there is little left to bind them together.

Ideal sexual partner: Purva Ashadha, the male monkey, finds its best sexual partner with the female monkey, Shravana. Both like their sex to be playful and fun. They enjoy each other's company sexually, and can develop their relationship into something more serious and committed.

Unsuitable sexual partners: Purva Ashadha are sexually incompatible with the sheep, Krittika and Pushya. Purva Ashadha look on their need for commitment as a sign of control and conformity. Purva Ashadha like sexual relationships to be fun; commitment is not part of their agenda. Krittika and Pushya in turn find them superficial. They never try to explore the deeper regions of each other's needs.
For complete relationship information, see pages 128–139.

CUSPS

Those born at the end or beginning of the Purva Ashadha should check the cusp details on page 142.

Uttara Ashadha

11 JANUARY TO 24 JANUARY

Key Words: Spiritual solitude

Ruled by: The Sun	
Symbol: Planks of a bed	
Animal sign: Mongoose	
Deity: Vishwadevas, the universal gods	
Motivation: Moksha	
Guna triplicity: Sattva, Rajas and Sattva	
Ayurvedic dosha: Kapha	
Colour: Copper	
Best direction: South	
Special consonants for birth names: Bea, Bo, Ja, Je	
Principal stars: Al-Baldah	
Western signs: Capricorn (11 to 20 January) and Aquarius (21 to 24 January)	

Symbol
PLANKS OF THE BED

The planks of the bed, the symbol of Uttara Ashadha, do not simply indicate a place for sleeping and resting. The planks indicate an austere bed, not one of comfort. Sleep is a necessary requirement to open our minds to its higher connections. Rest is used in yoga to relax the muscles so that the next asana can be taken slightly further. In the same way, Uttara Ashadha creates conditions so that the mind can relax and open itself to further wisdom and perception.

Meaning and Mythology

Uttara Ashadha is partly in Capricorn and partly in Aquarius. Saturn rules both. Vedic astrology uses traditional rulerships and does not recognize Uranus as the planetary ruler of Aquarius. Uttara Ashadha itself is ruled by the Sun. Consciousness is signified by the Sun and the influence of Saturn moves it towards a wholly different direction.

The animal symbol of Uttara Ashadha is the mongoose. There is no female mongoose in the nakshatras. This indicates that there are no ideal partners for Uttara Ashadha. In the animal kingdom the mongoose kills the snake. The snake here signifies our inner demons or darkness that have to be destroyed before an individual can move on.

'Uttara' means 'east' and 'Ashadha' means 'unsubdued'. It indicates what cannot be suppressed. The true nature of humans comes out regardless of what opposition they have to face. It is linked to the previous nakshatra, Purva Ashadha. Together they represent the common principle of unfolding new talents. In Purva Ashadha, there is a dawning of the new psychological changes taking place, but assimilation into the psyche actually happens in Uttara Ashadha.

Ruling deities

The ruling deities are the Vishwadevas, the universal gods who deliver their worshippers across the choppy waters of human life. They are also the gods who control the brain cells, promote social interaction and give harmonious physical conditions so that the inner person can develop. Uttara Ashadha concentrates on the mind and the intellectual development of the individual.

UTTARA ASHADHA AIM IS FOR MOKSHA

Uttara Ashadha make the real psychological adjustment towards moksha. Letting go of the ego and merging with universal consciousness becomes paramount to them. The change is so profound and the inner need to leave behind the cycle of unhappiness so strong, that Uttara Ashadha sometimes lose their knack of relating to this world.

GUNA TRIPLICITY: SATTVA, RAJAS AND SATTVA

Sattva dominates the psychology of Uttara Ashadha on the primary (physical) and tertiary (spiritual) levels.

There is never any doubt about the thinking of Uttara Ashadha: it is pure and idealistic. However, problems can arise if they become too self-righteous. Rajas on the secondary (mental) level keeps them searching and can create conflicts that make them question their aims for peace and calmness.

AYURVEDIC DOSHA IS KAPHA

Kapha is philosophical, spiritual and emotional, but can be blocked by the emotional mind. They may turn to food or shopping for emotional comfort. Uttara Ashadha are bright, but they need to be careful not to over-indulge, as this can dull their minds and create problems for them in other areas of their life.

Uttara Ashadha

CHARACTERISTICS/ PERSONALITY TRAITS

Uttara Ashadha are dynamic and intellectually gifted. They are leaders who will doggedly pursue their ambitions. They are extremely bright, but their kapha natures can make them self-indulgent and this can dull their inner faculties.

Uttara Ashadhas hate deception or underhand dealings of any kind. They will go after someone who they believe is cheating, and will not rest until they have destroyed them. They are formidable enemies against corruption of any kind. On this level, they can be fundamentalist. Uttara Ashadha must realize that reality and truth can mean different things to different people, and should try to be more flexible.

The moksha nakshatras all want to achieve the impossible dream and sometimes cannot accept present reality. Uttara Ashadha are no exception; they can reject themselves, their family and relationships, if they do not match up to their idealistic aspirations. This makes it difficult for them to live with others, but most importantly with themselves. They have tremendous heights to scale, but they can only do so if they are happy with themselves.

One of their most important characteristics is their need to be alone.

HOW IT LINKS WITH THE WESTERN SUN SIGN AND RULER

Uttara Ashadha in Capricorn: Capricorns choose to pay the price of their previous karma; Uttara Ashadha are aware of their spiritual responsibilities. This Sun/Saturn combination means there is both darkness and light, day and night, practical and spiritual.

Uttara Ashadha in Aquarius: Aquarius starts to work in accordance with the universal law and gives up individual identification; Uttara Ashadha signifies psychological changes in the individual. The inspirational nature of Uttara Ashadha means they are able to direct attention for the good of others, not for themselves.

SPIRITUAL LIFE PATH

Uttara Ashadha's spiritual life path is connected towards working practically towards their life ambitions. First, they have to work to fulfil their own ambitions; then they are in a position to go beyond their own desires. This can make them selfish to start with, but they will then change. From the selfishness will emerge an individual who is prepared to give and even to sacrifice their own needs for the good of others.

RELATIONSHIPS

Uttara Ashadha have extremely complicated relationship needs. All the symbolism connected to their nakshatra stands for being alone. Their nakshatra ruler, the Sun, is a loner. Saturn, their western sign ruler, stands for asceticism; their animal sign, the mongoose, does not have any companion among the other nakshatras. This gives Uttara Ashadha a difficult remit regarding their relationships. They will not be happy with the traditional relationships that society demands and must find one that works for them. In their relationships, they must have independence and quality time to pursue their own spirituality.

SEXUAL ENERGY LINKED TO THE MONGOOSE

The animal symbol of Uttara Ashadha is the mongoose. Relationships with snake nakshatras such as Rohini or Mrigasira should be avoided, as their instincts are to destroy each other. Sexually, Uttara Ashadha can be active and bold. If they are attracted to someone, they will make a play for them. They are quick workers and people can find themselves involved with Uttara Ashadha in no time at all. Uttara Ashadha play by different rules.

FAMOUS UTTARA ASHADHA

Cecil Beaton, Aristotle Onassis, Cary Grant, Anton Chekhov, Paul Cézanne, Federico Fellini.

HOW UTTARA ASHADHA RELATES TO OTHER NAKSHATRAS

Most compatible: Uttara Bhadra is the best relationship for Uttara Ashadha. Uttara Bhadra recognize the innate loneliness within Uttara Ashadha; their unconditional love thaws Uttara Ashadha's frozen inner core. Purva Ashadha also make good partners for Uttara Ashadha. They can create a perfect relationship even though they have completely different personalities.

Least compatible: With Magha they find the greatest obstacle as both are powerful nakshatras. This relationship can quickly become one of rivalry and a struggle for dominance. Uttara Ashadha's animal sign is the mongoose, Ashlesha's symbol and ruling deity are the serpents. The serpents and the mongoose are deadly rivals in nature, and this rivalry gets translated into the relationships between Ashlesha and Uttara Ashadha.

Ideal sexual partner: The mongoose has no female counterpart in the nakshatra system, suggesting that perfect sexual and emotional compatibility is not possible. Uttara Ashadha is a highly spiritual sign; the mind is being told to focus on matters beyond the sexual. This can create difficulty in finding an ideal sexual mate, but there are many nakshatras that have 75 per cent compatibility with them.

Unsuitable sexual partners: The snakes, Rohini and Mrigasira, are deadly enemies of the mongoose, so should be avoided. Even if other areas of life are compatible, the enmity will surface at some stage. It would require great self-control on both sides to make a relationship work.
For complete relationship information, see pages 128–139.

CUSPS

Those born at the end or beginning of the Uttara Ashadha should check the cusp details on pages 142–3.

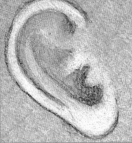

Shravana

24 JANUARY TO 6 FEBRUARY

Key Word: Sounds of silence

Ruled by: The Moon	
Symbol: Ear	
Animal sign: Monkey	
Deity: Vishnu, the preserver of the universe	
Motivation: Artha	
Guna triplicity: Sattva, Tamas and Rajas	
Ayurvedic dosha: Kapha	
Colour: Light blue	
Best direction: North	
Special consonants for birth names: Ju, Jay, Jo, Gha	
Principal stars: Altair	
Western signs: Aquarius	

Symbol
EAR

 The symbol of the ear assigned to Shravana further enhances its listening quality. In the Upanishad there is a prayer to grant the capacity to listen properly. When you learn to listen in the true sense of the word, you hear beyond the spoken word.

Meaning and Mythology

The Moon rules Shravana and the nakshatra is placed in Aquarius which is ruled by Saturn (Vedic astrology uses traditional rulerships and does not recognize Uranus as the ruler of Aquarius). This Saturn/Moon combination makes for a difficult situation. The Moon waxes and wanes and is emotional and changeable; Saturn is disciplined, rigid and inflexible.

'Shravana' means 'listening' and it is the nakshatra of total silence. To listen to the sounds of silence can only be done through self-discipline, yoga and the path of truth. This silence leads to the development of our ability to see through the illusions of life. This nakshatra indicates the need for quietness and reflection. The total silence of meditation leads to a better understanding within ourselves. To sit in silence we have to like ourselves; it forces us to recognize the truth and not hide within the cacophony of life. We need to assimilate these ideas and listen to what our inner self is telling us as well as what others have to say.

The Moon, the ruler of the nakshatra, signifies the ever-vacillating mind. It also is the controller of life on earth where nothing is certain. The mind has to learn the lesson of equilibrium and be at peace with itself. Our earthly instincts have also got to be regulated before we can reach a deeper understanding of the essence of life.

Ruling deities

Vishnu is the personification of all the 12 sun gods; therefore he represents the zodiac. He is also the light beyond our perception. 'Vishnu' is considered one of the most important gods of the Vedas. He forms the holy trinity with Shiva and Brahma. 'Vishnu' means 'he who crosses heights'. He encourages his followers to scale the heights beyond their capabilities.

SHRAVANA AIM IS FOR ARTHA

Shravana are goal-orientated and they focus on achievement. Their goals are connected to business, the building of wealth (both spiritual and material), and making an impact on the world around them. They are pragmatic and disciplined in their approach to life. Artha for Shravana means finding practical ways of doing service for the good of humanity.

GUNA TRIPLICITY: SATTVA, TAMAS AND RAJAS

The psychological quality of Shravana is the braiding of the three gunas. The physical life (Sattva) has to be led for the right reasons; the mind (Tamas) is blocking itself by insisting on a more material approach to life, and the spirit (Rajas) is lost in a search for its essence. In the right blend, the three gunas can create conditions for the rebirth of the soul. Tamas on the secondary (mental) level strongly indicates that Shravana has not fully completed its work on Earth to qualify for or want moksha.

AYURVEDIC DOSHA IS KAPHA

Shravana are philosophical, spiritual and emotional. Their emotions play an important role in their life, as they are trying to keep control of them. Shravana have to beware of self-indulgence – whether it is allowing themselves to be too emotional or over-eating for comfort.

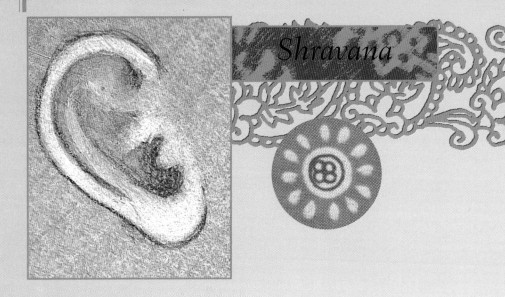

Shravana

CHARACTERISTICS/ PERSONALITY TRAITS

Shravana are extremely intelligent, and are often bordering on genius. They have sharp and incisive minds. If they are true to their nakshatra they will learn to control their minds and begin to draw from within.

Most Shravana thirst for silence and moments of peace amidst the noise of life. In today's world the noise of piped music, televisions and traffic make such an impact on our lives, that we forget to trust in silence. Shravana need to connect with this desire for silence. If they do so, they will start feeding their soul. In India people perform a fast that is known as 'Maun Vrat', fasting from speaking. By keeping quiet, they are able to hear.

This ability to listen means Shravana can hear the voice of the people. They will make good politicians and community leaders. Shravana are usually experts at dealing with other people's problems. They need to be of service to others. If they cannot achieve this through their work, they should do it in their spare time, undertaking voluntary work for charities or helping those in need.

Shravana may appear hard on the outside, but underneath they are emotional and sentimental. They can develop a shell to hide their emotional natures. They tend to live in a world of their own, but although they are dreamers, they can still be tough and resilient.

HOW IT LINKS WITH THE WESTERN SUN SIGN AND RULER

Shravana in Aquarius: Aquarius is called Kumbha in Sanskrit. Kumbhaka is the practice of controlling the breath in yoga, which helps us to control the mind. Shravana's ruler, the Moon, signifies the mind. At Shravana, we learn to still the mind so that we can master our emotions.

SPIRITUAL LIFE PATH

Shravana's spiritual path is connected to letting go of their selfish desires and working for others; protecting their rights and caring for their needs. Shravana have to work in the world, although they desire to move towards a more spiritual place. Shravana have the ability to look beyond what ordinary people aspire towards.

RELATIONSHIPS

Shravana are highly emotional, but they may not show it. They find it difficult to say what they really feel, although they deeply desire a partner who will recognize their gentle nature and love them for what they are. Shravana who learn to control their minds will be able to detach themselves from this world, and become very self-dependent. Anyone who wants to be close to Shravana will have to love them on their terms, understand their emotional struggle, and not interpret their need to be alone as a personal insult or lack of love.

SEXUAL ENERGY LINKED TO THE FEMALE MONKEY

Monkeys are usually sociable, full of fun and the joys of the world, and like to live within a family unit. They are eager and playful, and can be very naughty. This is a side of their personality that Shravana rarely put on show.

Those who get involved with Shravana will see this light-hearted side of their personalities. They will be charming and impish. They like to fool around and they may not take sex too seriously. If they do not find a partner they are truly happy with, they can be sexually promiscuous.

FAMOUS SHRAVANA

Neil Diamond, Paul Newman, Wolfgang Amadeus Mozart, Clark Gable.

HOW SHRAVANA RELATES TO OTHER NAKSHATRAS

Most compatible: Uttara Bhadra is the best relationship for Shravana. They are loving and supportive, understand Shravana's moods, and accept them for what they are. With Bharani, the relationship is full of passion, and with Pushya, Uttara Bhadra find happiness from shared goals. Pushya and Shravana are not sexually compatible, but in other areas their compatibility is so good that if they work on the sexual side of their relationship, they can find complete happiness.

Least compatible: Magha is the most difficult relationship for Shravana. Shravana are sensitive and they feel rejected by Magha. Shravana need to develop thicker skins, while Magha need to be more caring and understand that a few careless words can damage their relationship with Shravana beyond repair.

Ideal sexual partner: Shravana's best sexual partner is the male monkey, Purva Ashadha. They will create fun and joy in their sexual relationship, and can understand each other's needs.

Unsuitable sexual partners: The monkey, Shravana, is sexually incompatible with Krittika and Pushya, the sheep. Shravana see their need for commitment as a sign of control. Shravana like sexual relationships to be fun; commitment is not part of their agenda. Krittika and Pushya in turn find them superficial. With Pushya, Shravana may be able to overcome the sexual incompatibility as this relationship works well in other areas, but with Krittika it is much more complicated.

For complete relationship information, see pages 128–139.

CUSPS

Those born at the end or beginning of the Shravana should check the cusp details on page 143.

Dhanishta

Key Words: Music

Ruled by: Mars	
Symbol: Flute or drum	
Animal sign: Lion	
Deity: The Eight Vasus	
Motivation: Dharma	
Guna triplicity: Sattva, Tamas and Tamas	
Ayurvedic dosha: Pitta	
Colour: Silver	
Best direction: East	
Special consonants for birth names: Ga, Ge, Go, Gay	
Principal stars: Sa'd-as-Suud	
Western signs: Aquarius	

Meaning and Mythology

Dhanishta is placed in Aquarius, ruled by Saturn (Vedic astrology uses traditional rulerships and does not recognize Uranus as the ruler of Aquarius). Mars rules Dhanishta. Mars and Saturn are opposing energies: one represents bravery and action and the other stands for restrictions. When Mars and Saturn conjunct, it is usually considered to be a warlike formation. The war in this case is being fought between the material and the spiritual self.

'Dhani' means 'wealthy' and 'Ishta' means 'complete'. Therefore 'Dhanishta' means 'complete wealth'. In ancient texts when the sages alluded to a person being wealthy, they meant that they had a wealth of good character, thoughts and actions. This was considered far superior to material wealth. Dhanishta has the blessing of wealth on every level. This wealth does not come easily to Dhanishta, but through selfless hard work, letting go of their personal egos, and acting with compassion and idealism for universal good.

Dhanishta represents the inner cleansing of the soul, which enables it to receive divine music. Many great philosophers and yogis are born under this sign, for example Lord Krishna, the great Indian god who gave his divine message in the Bhagavad Gita.

Symbol
DRUM OR FLUTE

Dhanishta is connected to the symbols of the drum and the flute – Shiva's drum or Krishna's flute. The symbol of the drum or the flute implies it is beating to the rhythm of someone else; others are to play their song through this drum. Both the drum and the flute are hollow inside and this indicates an emptiness within the Dhanishta person unless he finds something to fill it. Sometimes this can be a fruitless chasing of dreams. Dhanishta usually have a talent for music.

Ruling deities

 Vasus are the eight person-ifications of the Sun; they are Apas, Dhruva, Soma, Dhara, Anila, Anala, Pratyusha and Prabhas. These deities have a strong connection with the Sun and appear at different stages of manifestation to guide the soul towards its true direction. They are guiding Dhanishta from the end of their earthly journey to the start of their journey towards the divine.

DHANISHTA AIM IS FOR DHARMA

The motivation of dharma is at its most potent at this stage. Shri Krishna taught dharma to Arjuna in Bhagavad Gita, 'the divine song' that is the essence of the Vedas. The setting of Bhagavad Gita is a battlefield and the war is against his family. But on a spiritual level, Arjuna's war with his relatives is the war we fight every day when we are trying to conquer our desires, feelings and temptations. Lord Krishna guides Arjuna towards his duty – dharma that is his destiny. This is the essence of dharma for Dhanishta.

GUNA TRIPLICITY: SATTVA, TAMAS AND TAMAS

The psychological quality of Dhanishta are the two polarities of Sattva on the primary (physical) level and Tamas on the secondary (mental) and tertiary (spiritual) ones. This is a major struggle for Dhanishta. They are aware that their path is connected with truth and compassion for others, but Tamas on the mental level stops their mind and soul from completing this task fully. When the gunas become concentrated, the soul is developing so that it can embrace the next step of consciousness.

AYURVEDIC DOSHA IS KAPHA

Pitta is the fire in the belly that provides fuel for Dhanishta to operate. They are inspired, active and goal orientated. They want to burn away all that is superfluous from their life so that they are able to move on to the next level of development. Pitta need to be careful to control the fire, or they will burn away even what was useful to them.

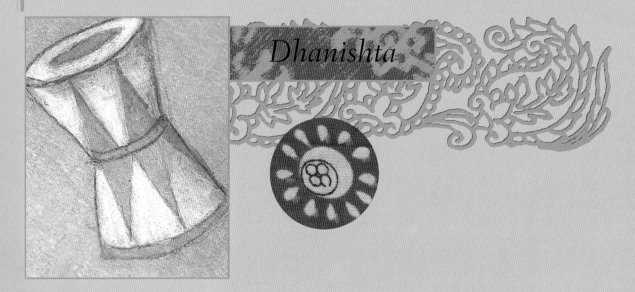

Dhanishta

CHARACTERISTICS/ PERSONALITY TRAITS

Dhanishta are a specially blessed nakshatra. They have tremendous ability to be spiritual while still being involved practically with worldly matters. Dhanishta are extremely charismatic and luminous. They can be strong in action, mind or word, and are leaders in whatever field they choose.

They have a selflessness that is not visible in any other nakshatra. They have moved a step further from Shravana. They are learning to both listen and speak; they work in the cacophony of life while also connecting to the supreme silence.

They live by the dictum 'not what others can do for me, but what I can do for others'. This is a wonderful achievement, but working in the world can bring problems for Dhanishta. They can only value themselves if they are actively involved in charitable concerns and helping others.

This is why it is important for Dhanishta, whatever their other pursuits, to involve themselves in giving of some sort. It does not have to be financial: a few hours helping a local charity or sitting with an elderly neighbour is just as valuable.

Dhanishta can become entangled in other people's ambitions. They can find themselves trying to fulfil the ambitions of other people, such as their parents or families.

HOW IT LINKS WITH THE WESTERN SUN SIGN AND RULER

Dhanishta in Aquarius: The symbol of Aquarius is a pitcher holding water. The pitcher represents the ego that restricts the growth of an individual. Dhanishta/Aquarius have to work to break the pitcher so that the water can flow freely and the individual can connect to the universal force.

SPIRITUAL LIFE PATH

Dhanishta's spiritual path is connecting to selfless service to humanity. To do this, they have to empty their souls of desires and make themselves pure within. This state is usually achieved after painful experiences. Dhanishta learn to let go of their egos and become a conduit for higher powers that can be used for the good of humanity.

RELATIONSHIPS

Dhanishta will be charismatic and strong, yet there are always invisible barriers in their relationships, both intimate and impersonal.

If Dhanishta can find someone who meets their high expectations, they will be loyal partners. They see everything in life as a responsibility, and that includes their partners. They are usually lucky with their relationships because people will tolerate a lot from Dhanishta.

SEXUAL ENERGY LINKED TO THE LIONESS

The lioness hunts side by side with the lion. They are strong and exemplify female power. They live in wild open places and are masters of all they survey.

All of the above are applicable to Dhanishta. They will be very much in charge of their own sexuality. If they are attracted to someone, they will make it obvious. Dhanishta have a strong sexual appetite. They enjoy sex and once satiated they may not look for another sexual encounter until they are ready for it.

Dhanishta will remain faithful as long as their partners do the same. If their partners stray, so will they. They do not believe in double standards at all.

FAMOUS DHANISHTA

Charles Dickens, Mia Farrow, Jules Verne, John McEnroe, Galileo Galilei.

Dhanishta are not possessive. They may not be willing to commit and do not necessarily expect commitment from you.

HOW DHANISHTA RELATES TO OTHER NAKSHATRAS

Most compatible: Shatabhishak are the best partners for Dhanishta. On the face of it, this relationship may seem unsuitable, but Dhanishta love Shatabhishak's intensity and Shatabhishak are able to project their inner desires through Dhanishta. With Krittika, it is an alliance between two powerful people. Both enjoy and respect each other's strength, but are able to retain their own individual personalities.

Least compatible: Uttara Bhadra is the worst relationship for Dhanishta. Dhanishta need a lover who is regal and powerful. Uttara Bhadra's nature is giving and egalitarian. Dhanishta can become distant, cold, and, ultimately, easily bored with their Uttara Bhadra partners.

Ideal sexual partner: The lioness Dhanishta needs the male lion, Purva Bhadra, to satisfy her sexual needs. Both are powerful and strong; they can commit sexually to each other. This can be an exciting and sensual relationship.

Unsuitable sexual partners: Dhanishta are sexually incompatible with the elephants, Bharani and Revati. Elephants and lions are both powerful creatures in the animal kingdom and are naturally hostile. This enmity is translated in sexual relationships. With Revati, there is a possibility of having a relationship, but as Bharani are also incompatible in every other area of life, this relationship is very difficult.

For complete relationship information, see pages 128–139.

CUSPS

Those born at the end or beginning of the Dhanishta should check the cusp details on page 143.

Shatabhishak

19 FEBRUARY TO 4 MARCH

Key Word: Insight

Ruled by: Rahu	
Symbol: Hundred stars	
Animal sign: Horse	
Deity: Varuna, the god of sea	
Motivation: Dharma	
Guna triplicity: Sattva, Tamas and Sattva	
Ayurvedic dosha: Vata	
Colour: Aquamarine	
Best direction: South	
Special consonants for birth names: Go, Sa, Se, So	
Principal stars: Sa'd-al-Akhbiyah	
Western signs: Aquarius (19 February) and Pisces (20 February to 4 March)	

Meaning and Mythology

Shatabhishak is the final nakshatra ruled by Rahu. A small part of it is placed in Aquarius, ruled by Saturn, and the rest is in Pisces, ruled by Jupiter. (Vedic astrology uses traditional rulerships and does not recognize Uranus and Neptune as the rulers here.) Pisces' symbol is the fish. A fish cannot survive out of water; for Pisces it means having to merge their individuality into cosmic forces. Rahu impacts the mind and creates massive spiritual blocks towards inner growth for Shatabhishak. When the task becomes difficult, Jupiter as the supreme guru is there to guide and help us with his wisdom.

'Shat' means 'hundred' and 'bhishak' means 'demons and healers'. Shatabhishak have special healing properties. Shatabhishak can be both demonic and godly, indicating the two sides of man; one has to be conquered to find the other. Shatabhishak is connected to the sage Valmiki who, according to the Vedas, was a robber before he found the true path. Valmiki is credited with writing the great epic Ramayana, which tells the story of the victory of good over evil through the story of Rama, the pious prince and Ravana, the demon king.

In Shatabhishak, the mind will set up mental obstacles that have to be mastered before the soul can let go of its ego.

Symbol
THE HUNDRED STARS

Shatabhishak's symbol is the hundred stars that are said to resemble the thousand-petal flower, indicating the Crown chakra. The hundred stars show the deep connection of Shatabhishak to the cosmos and past karma. The stars are supposed to be silent watchers of the play of life. The flowering of the thousand-petal flower indicates the complete flowering of inner beauty. The flower blooms for the joy of others; it does not recognize its own beauty.

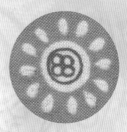

Ruling deities

The presiding deity is Varuna, the ancient Vedic god who rules the oceans and directs the sun and wind. He is said to have extraordinary powers to heal and rejuvenate through the use of physic herbs and medicine. He can prevent death and destruction. As the god of the oceans he controls the emotions and the mind, and so he has the ability to bestow wisdom and change the direction of the mind.

SHATABHISHAK AIM IS FOR DHARMA

This is the last nakshatra to reflect the motivation of dharma, which is now at its final intensity. Shatabhishak know about doing the right thing; they have gone beyond the stage of Dhanishta. They have fought the battle with their desires and won, they have learnt to let go of their egos. The dharma here is connected to doing the right thing by themselves. They know that what lies in the path of their final realization is their own minds.

GUNA TRIPLICITY: SATTVA, TAMAS AND SATTVA

The psychological qualities of Shatabhishak are the two polarities of Sattva on the primary (physical) and tertiary (spiritual) levels, and Tamas on the secondary (mental) level. Rahu controls the Tamas guna. It creates psychological problems: Rahu's domain makes Shatabhishak pull away from its pure self. This Tamas has to be seen as the last mental block before true perception is able to dawn, and it is the most difficult one. This is why Shatabhishak are sometimes tempted to do what is patently wrong for them, taking a path of self-destruction.

AYURVEDIC DOSHA IS VATA

Shatabhishak have nervous dispositions. Their restlessness can create both physical and mental stress. This sign is so connected to psychological blocks that vata further aggravates it. The mind is in such a hurry to find the answers, that too much energy is whizzing around the brain. Vata needs to be calmed; otherwise, there may be mental overload.

Shatabhishak

CHARACTERISTICS/ PERSONALITY TRAITS

Shatabhishak have strong principles. They must accept that they are still human and should try to deal with any impediments blocking their path. Shatabhishak can be secretive. If they keep their weaknesses to themselves, it can create more problems at a later date. They may reveal their secret weakness at some stage, but still try to hold onto their whiter-than-white façade.

Shatabhishak have the ability to achieve the impossible. They can set themselves impossible targets and will go beyond even their own goals. They have sharp minds and are usually highly perceptive.

However, Shatabhishak lack self-confidence. They are like flowers that do not recognize their own beauty, so they will be perpetually disappointed by their achievements. They must try to look within themselves to find happiness, and stop equating purely material gains with success. This will help them to untangle their inner conundrums and enable them to detach themselves from their worldly successes and failures.

HOW IT LINKS WITH THE WESTERN SUN SIGN AND RULER

Shatabhishak in Aquarius: Aquarius is ruled by Saturn and Rahu's rulership of the nakshatra makes for a difficult combination. Life has to have a purpose and the overall direction is about learning lessons. Rahu gives results like Saturn, but on a psychological level. This double Saturnine influence is difficult to handle unless activities are directed towards service to humanity.

Shatabhishak in Pisces: Pisces deals with merging the individual into the universal; Shatabhishak symbolizes the heavenly ocean. Both are connected to the mind and emotions. This nakshatra is about understanding the power of the mind and allowing it to go beyond ordinary perception.

SPIRITUAL LIFE PATH

Shatabhishak's spiritual life path is concerned with letting the mind merge with the consciousness. A clever mind sometimes becomes an impediment to understanding the infinite forces of nature, as it limits its intelligence to the perception of the present.

Shatabhishak's spiritual path is linked to letting go of their individuality, allowing their minds to expand and to venture into the unknown.

HOW SHATABHISHAK RELATES TO OTHER NAKSHATRAS

Most compatible: Dhanishta are the best partners for Shatabhishak, who have a very private nature but can be open with Dhanishta. Other Shatabhishak are also good relationships for them. They understand each other's personalities and instinctively create conditions for long-term partnerships. Shatabhishak can also enjoy good relationships with Rohini and Krittika.

Least compatible: Punarvasu is the worst relationship for Shatabhishak. Punarvasu find it difficult to understand Shatabhishak's inner nature, while Shatabhishak find Punarvasu's love superficial. They never give each other a chance to express their love properly. Hasta can be very possessive and demanding; Shatabhishak find their inability to return these emotions unsettling. They should be open about the fact that their definition of love includes independence and self-reliance.

Ideal sexual partner: The female horse, Shatabhishak, finds sexual happiness with the male horse, Ashwini. Both are too independent to make the relationship work in other areas of life unless they learn to respect each other's individuality.

Unsuitable sexual partners: The buffalos, Hasta and Swati, are never fully sexually confident and therefore they don't project the sexual aura necessary to keep Shatabhishak interested. With Hasta, relationship compatibility in other areas is not good, so it will be more difficult for Shatabhishak to make this relationship work than one with Swati. *For complete relationship information, see pages 128–139.*

CUSPS

Those born at the end or beginning of the Shatabhishak should check the cusp details on page 143.

RELATIONSHIPS

Shatabhishak are a real contradiction. They may appear to be traditional and pious, yet they need relationships that are non-traditional and exciting. In the society of ancient India, this created great difficulties. Often the relationship they wanted was so different from the one that society expected of them, that they chose to remain single. In the more relaxed environment of today's society, Shatabhishak do not have to face such a difficult dilemma. However, problems can arise when they are not open about their desires and build up a secret network of relationships. This can become one of the inner blocks that hinder them in achieving their life's ambitions – spiritual or material.

SEXUAL ENERGY LINKED TO THE FEMALE HORSE

Shatabhishak are the female horse. Female stands for passivity. Horses are beautiful, proud and majestic, but they also have nervous temperaments. Shatabhishak can be fearful and highly strung and will find it difficult to trust others with their sexual desires. They may have strong sexual urges, but they will hardly ever express these openly and will never take the initiative.

FAMOUS SHATABHISHAK

George Frideric Handel, Wilhelm Grimm, Pierre Auguste Renoir, Elizabeth Taylor.

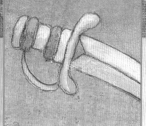

Purva Bhadra

4 March to 17 March

Key Words: Peace and ideology

Ruled by: Jupiter	
Symbol: Sword	
Animal sign: Lion	
Deity: Aja Ekapada, the one-footed goat	
Motivation: Artha	
Guna triplicity: Sattva, Sattva and Rajas	
Ayurvedic dosha: Vata	
Colour: Silver	
Best direction: West	
Special consonants for birth names: Say, So, Da, De	
Principal stars: Al-Fargh-Al-Mukdim	
Western signs: Pisces	

Meaning and Mythology

Purva Bhadra is in Pisces. Jupiter rules both. Jupiter expands and pushes through new frontiers. Pisces is the stage of merging the individual consciousness with the universal one. Purva Bhadra stands for stability, courage and change. Idealism is the essence of this nakshatra. It wants to change the world and fight for its cause regardless of the consequences.

Purva Bhadra is connected to the following nakshatra, Uttara Bhadra. 'Purva' means 'west' and 'Bhadra' means 'beautiful'. This is where the true beauty of an individual can emerge. This is not physical beauty, but the beauty that shines through a person as a direct result of inner perfection. (See also Uttara Bhadra.)

Purva Bhadra relates to the position where the meaning of life has been revealed and understood. It teaches the lesson of being at peace within one's self, and leading a life with no expectation of personal rewards, glorification or ambitions.

Symbol
SWORD

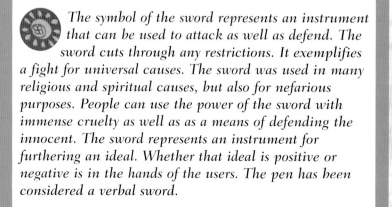

The symbol of the sword represents an instrument that can be used to attack as well as defend. The sword cuts through any restrictions. It exemplifies a fight for universal causes. The sword was used in many religious and spiritual causes, but also for nefarious purposes. People can use the power of the sword with immense cruelty as well as as a means of defending the innocent. The sword represents an instrument for furthering an ideal. Whether that ideal is positive or negative is in the hands of the users. The pen has been considered a verbal sword.

Ruling deities

 The ruling deity is Aja Ekapada, the one-footed goat. 'Aja' means 'the unborn'; 'Eka' means 'one'; and 'pada' means 'feet'. The goat gives milk, it lives alone and is silent or unborn. A goat may not be necessarily physically attractive, but it reveals its beauty by supporting life.

Aja Ekapada relates to infinity, where there is no sound or motion, but an outward stillness with creative energies bubbling underneath.

PURVA BHADRA AIM IS FOR ARTHA

Artha usually means work or wealth-creating activities. Another meaning of artha is the answer. Purva Bhadra look beyond the artha of the earthly life and search for answers in the cosmos. Purva Bhadra will also be good at practical expression of artha; their main motivation will be with the spiritual.

GUNA TRIPLICITY: SATTVA, SATTVA AND RAJAS

The psychological qualities of Purva Bhadra are Sattva on the primary (physical) and secondary (mental) levels and Rajas on the tertiary (spiritual). Rajas on the spiritual level shows the interplay of cosmic forces searching to express themselves. The outward self of Purva Bhadra is pure; the mind is still. There is action in the passivity. The individual appears calm and in tune with themselves, but their inner self is full of kinetic currents waiting to be expressed.

AYURVEDIC DOSHA IS VATA

Vata is discontentment, inconsistency, and agitation. Purva Bhadra keep their tensions and conflicts buried deep within themselves. They are worriers and fret mostly about worldly issues: the environment, injustice and truth. They will rarely worry about themselves. Every day they can find a new issue to consume their inner energy. They use up their entire fund of resources for the good of humanity.

Purva Bhadra

CHARACTERISTICS/ PERSONALITY TRAITS

Purva Bhadra are calm and placid until you get them onto the topic of the world's injustice. They usually have pet projects and support many worthwhile charities. They have strong and powerful views on prejudice, cruelty and oppression. They are willing to sacrifice their time, money and even their careers to fight for their beliefs. They are excellent campaigners and friends will always be surprised at how such calm and passive people can suddenly become so impasssioned.

Purva Bhadra is one of the most caring nakshatras. They are always ready to help others and people usually flock to them for advice. This is one of the reasons why Purva Bhadra can feel depleted. Their friends, relatives and acquaintances can use up too much of their energy with constant demands.

Purva Bhadra are good writers. They can use the pen like a sword to fight against atrocities and injustices. They are also imaginative and therefore make brilliant fictional writers, too.

Material success does not make them any good at handling money. They should have strong financial plans in place, and be careful about how they invest their money and who they trust with it. Purva Bhadra genuinely do not care what happens to their money, and they can be suckers for ideas and plans that seem too good to be true.

HOW IT LINKS WITH THE WESTERN SUN SIGN AND RULER

Purva Bhadra in Pisces: Pisces deals with merging the individual into the universal; Purva Bhadra share this principle. These people work in harmony with their outer karma. They aim to create a perfect spiritual life where their immense light shines brightly and success or failure in their material life become irrelevant.

SPIRITUAL LIFE PATH

Purva Bhadra are spirituality itself. Their path is connected with giving. How they will do this is left to them. Their karma is compassion, kindness and the fight against injustice. Their outer self is connected to the purity of Sattva, reflecting its beneficence for the good of all; the selflessness of Jupiter, giving without expectation of return; and finally, Aja Ekapada, the silent one-footed goat who sustains others while being totally self-reliant.

RELATIONSHIPS

Purva Bhadra will usually only see the positive in any relationship. They have a tendency to see their partners through rose-tinted glasses and may be cheated on because it takes them so long to realize the truth about the other person.

Relationships are important to Purva Bhadra and they will invest a great amount of emotional energy in them. They are seeking a relationship that will make them feel complete. They are good spouses, parents and friends. Purva Bhadra are very emotional and tend to live in a world of their own. They can appear to be dependent, but in fact they are extremely self-reliant and strong.

SEXUAL ENERGY LINKED TO THE LION

The lion is the king of the jungle, its long, flowing mane symbolizing power and strength. These proud and beautiful beasts dominate the animal kingdom.

All of the above are applicable to Purva Bhadra. Male or female, they have strong personalities, are dynamic and virile, and are sexually potent. They can be arrogant; they believe they only have to show an interest in a member of the opposite sex, and they will get them. They are calm and gentle only if life is going the way they like.

FAMOUS PURVA BHADRA

Michelangelo, Yuri Gagarin, Michael Caine, Jerry Lewis, Rudolf Nureyev.

HOW PURVA BHADRA RELATES TO OTHER NAKSHATRAS

Most compatible: Purva Bhadra do not experience great highs or lows in their relationships. Purva Bhadra's ruler, Jupiter, gives them the wisdom to work at relationships. Their best one is with Uttara Bhadra, whose giving nature makes them ideal for the loving Purva Bhadra. As two halves of the same constellation, they represent different expressions of the same principle. Mrigasira is another partner that Purva Bhadra will find intellectually and emotionally fulfilling.

Least compatible: Purva Bhadra find relationships with Jyeshta the most painful. Jyeshta express contradictory traits of sensuality and asceticism. Purva Ashadha try hard to love them, but they are too far apart intellectually, and Jyeshta can be unreliable. Purva Bhadra have the ability to bring out the best in other people, so they will usually work at even the most difficult of partnerships.

Ideal sexual partner: The lioness, Dhanishta, is the best partner to satisfy the sexual needs of the male lion, Purva Bhadra. Both are loyal and powerful. They will be able to make a long-term commitment to each other as well.

Unsuitable sexual partners: Purva Bhadra are sexually incompatible with the elephants, Bharani and Revati. Elephants and lions are both powerful creatures in the animal kingdom and are naturally hostile. Bharani and Revati challenge Purva Bhadra's power and this is translated in sexual relationships. This underlying power struggle will always make these partnerships difficult.
For complete relationship information, see pages 128–139.

CUSPS

Those born at the end or beginning of the Purva Bhadra should check the cusp details on page 143.

Uttara Bhadra

17 MARCH TO 31 MARCH

Key Words: Beautiful darkness

Ruled by: Saturn	
Symbol: Twins	
Animal sign: Cow	
Deity: Ahir Budhyana	
Motivation: Kama	
Guna triplicity: Sattva, Sattva and Tamas	
Ayurvedic dosha: Pitta	
Colour: Purple	
Best direction: North	
Special consonants for birth names: Du, Tha, Aa, Jna	
Principal stars: Al-Pargh-Al-Mukdim	
Western signs: Pisces (17 to 20 March) and Aries (21 to 31 March)	

Symbol
TWINS

The symbol of the twins shows the duality of Uttara Ashadha. Uttara Ashadha lose interest in life, yet have to live successfully in this world. Uttara Ashadha represents duality in every form: it has found light so it must go into darkness; it is sattvic, therefore it embraces Tamas. The twins reflect the splitting of the atom, the gravitational pull of the earth – all the polarities of Uttara Phalguni make this nakshatra extremely complex and full of intuitive energies.

Meaning and Mythology

Uttara Bhadra is partly in Pisces, ruled by Jupiter, and partly in Aries, ruled by Mars. Its ruler is Saturn. Saturn is linked to resistance, difficulties and opposition in the beginning, but harmony at the end. Jupiter and Mars both show contrary aspects. Jupiter gives the wisdom to face adversity and Mars brings courage. No spiritual journey is ever complete without Martian courage. Pisces is the end of the spiritual journey and Aries the beginning. For a spiritual journey to be complete it should go full circle: the beginning is linked to the end. This is what is taking place in Uttara Bhadra.

Uttara Bhadra is an extension of the previous nakshatra, Purva Bhadra. The two Bhadras form a singular principle that is split into two opposing forces which constitute the universe. Purva is ruled by Jupiter and Uttara by Saturn. Together they represent darkness and light, fire and water, heat and cold, masculine and feminine, the lion and the cow. Purva Bhadra's deity, Aja Ekapada, reflects the Sun and Uttara Bhadra's deity, Ahir Bhudnya, is the Moon. Jupiter bestows wisdom in Purva Bhadra, and Saturn rewards all the trials and tribulations in Uttara Bhadra.

'Uttara' means 'east' and 'Bhadra' means 'beautiful'. Uttara Bhadra indicates a journey to a beautiful place. This nakshatra deals with both the end and the beginning. An individual reaches a particular point in life where they merge their consciousness with the darkness of the sky; everything becomes one. Out of this mysterious darkness all forms of creation emerge; day breaks at the end of the night.

Ruling deities

Ahir Budhnya is linked to Soma, the Moon god. It is associated with water and darkness. The passivity of darkness is the mysterious source from which all forms of creation have arisen. Ahir Budhnya, the deep-ocean snake, represents the merging of consciousness with the deep sea of eternity. The serpent also symbolizes wisdom. The snake shedding its skin represents rebirth and the cycles of life.

UTTARA BHADRA AIM IS FOR KAMA

The motivation of kama or passion is not connected to sexual passion, but to the intense desire to merge with the unconscious, and to use their talents for the good of humanity. This passion and dynamism is reflected spiritually.

GUNA TRIPLICITY: SATTVA, SATTVA AND TAMAS

The psychological qualities of Uttara Bhadra are the two polarities of Sattva on the primary (physical) and secondary (mental) levels and Tamas on the tertiary (spiritual) one. Tamas is always described as darkness, and here the darkness of the abstract level is of nothingness, of totality where neither good nor bad is visible. The soul submerges into this mysterious dark force, so that it can begin another journey, but for Uttara Phalguni the expression is total stillness. The important factor is that Uttara Bhadra voluntarily embraces Tamas or darkness; it returns to where it began.

AYURVEDIC DOSHA IS PITTA

Pitta people are adventurous and determined. Uttara Ashadha use this dosha to take them into the sea of the unknown. Pitta gives them the dynamism to do this. There is no nervousness of vata or the philosophy and laid back approach of kapha. Pitta people use their grit and determination to make the impossible happen.

Uttara Bhadra

CHARACTERISTICS/ PERSONALITY TRAITS

Uttara Bhadra carry within them profound wisdom. It has nothing to do with how highly they are educated. From the moment they are born, they have a sense of destiny, a feeling of detachment from life. These feelings may become blocks for Uttara Bhadra when they are younger. They may be at odds with the burgeoning feelings of spirituality within them. They should not ignore them; when the time is right, they will naturally grow towards them.

They will be egalitarian and will treat every one equally regardless of colour, creed and status. They are idealistic and they will respect your dreams, too. They are compassionate and charitable. Like the cow, their animal sign, they will nourish others and not think only of themselves.

They are knowledgeable and wise. This is why they make good teachers and advisers. They want to pass on their knowledge and nourish the minds of others so that they in turn can prosper. Uttara Bhadra do not have any selfish motive. The act of giving becomes the food for their soul. On the negative side, they can become lazy and overweight.

They may be irresponsible and can get involved in the wrong type of company.

HOW IT LINKS WITH THE WESTERN SUN SIGN AND RULER

Uttara Bhadra in Pisces: Pisces is at the end of the journey and Uttara Bhadra are making a beautiful journey of life. They are spiritual, at one with their emotional needs. If their outer life is harmonized with their inner needs they will experience very little conflict.

Uttara Bhadra in Aries: Uttara Bhadra and Aries show the beginning of spiritual journeys. Uttara Bhadra reflects twin principles and Aries connects with the second part of this journey. It provides the courage and the strength to progress towards a difficult goal.

SPIRITUAL LIFE PATH

Uttara Bhadra's spiritual path is connected to living life successfully on earth but becoming detached from it. The state of being attached to the material pleasures of life has ended, but the completion of the path to enlightenment is still continuing. The soul endeavours to complete the circle of one manifestation.

RELATIONSHIPS

Uttara Bhadra are highly emotional. They want an ideal relationship and will work hard to achieve this. However, if their relationship does not prosper, they will move on or live alone. There are two distinct sides to their personality: they may be sensual and loving, but they can also be detached, spiritual and ascetic. They shift from one personality to the other. Although they are usually good with children, they may decide not to have their own.

SEXUAL ENERGY LINKED TO THE COW

This is a vital sign. The cow is sacred in India. The sexual act has always been considered as sacred expression of love for one's partner. The kamdhenu, a special sacred cow, had the ability to fulfil all desires. In the same way, sexuality properly expressed can fulfil a person.

People of Uttara Bhadra nakshatra do not care whether they are sexually active or not. They may want love, relationships and sex, but if none of these are available, they can learn to live without them.

FAMOUS UTTARA BHADRA

Johann Sebastian Bach, Joan Crawford, Elton John, Steve McQueen.

HOW UTTARA BHADRA RELATES TO OTHER NAKSHATRAS

Most compatible: Revati is the best partner for Uttara Bhadra. Both are idealistic; they find a perfect companion in each other and will work hard to keep their relationship loving. Uttara Bhadra recognize the innate loneliness within Uttara Ashadha; they take the time to work at developing this relationship. Uttara Bhadra and Purva Bhadra express themselves differently in relationships, but they have similar natures and outlooks.

Least compatible: Bharani is the most difficult relationship for Uttara Bhadra. Uttara Bhadra are spiritual and Bharani are sensual; their life paths have no meeting ground. This can create real unhappiness in the long run if they do not try to understand each other's nature. Chitra can hurt Uttara Bhadra, and their sexual incompatibility makes this relationship frustrating and disappointing on many levels.

Ideal sexual partner: Uttara Phalguni, the bull, is the best sexual mate for the cow, Uttara Bhadra. Their rational hardworking exteriors hide an earthy sensuality. They are natural sexual partners and will bring happiness to each other.

Unsuitable sexual partners: The worst sexual partners for Uttara Bhadra are the tigers, Chitra and Vishakha. Uttara Bhadra find it difficult to trust Chitra and Vishakha. They need commitment and loyalty, which Chitra and Vishakha are not always willing to give.

For complete relationship information, see pages 128–139.

CUSPS

Those born at the end or beginning of the Uttara Bhadra should check the cusp details on page 143.

Revati

31 MARCH TO 13 APRIL

Key Words: Purity

Ruled by: Mercury	
Symbol: Fish	
Animal sign: Elephant	
Deity: Pushan, a sun god	
Motivation: Moksha	
Guna triplicity: Sattva, Sattva and Sattva	
Ayurvedic dosha: Kapha	
Colour: Brown	
Best direction: East	
Special consonants for birth names: De, Do, Chaa, Chee	
Principal stars: Batn-Al-Hut	
Western signs: Pisces (17 to 20 March) and Aries (21 to 31 March)	

Meaning and Mythology

In Revati the seed is sown for fruition at a later date. The celestial messenger, Mercury, rules Revati. Being the last nakshatra of the zodiac, Revati is powerful in realizing the ultimate truths about life, death, transformation and change. The experience of Revati changes our way of thinking towards a higher, deeper prospective.

'Revati' means 'abundant' or 'wealthy' and Revati's wealth is connected to spiritual wealth. Revati is connected to wealth because the crops were usually harvested at the time when the Sun was in Revati nakshatra, and thus the ancient sages felt the beneficence of Revati.

Saturn was born under Revati. Saturn represents time and duration, and the Sun, his father, stands for infinity. The birth of time by infinity highlights an important aspect of Revati – that within the universal soul is the individual soul. With birth lies death; the individual is nothing but a reflection of the absolute. Revati is entirely in the sign of Aries which indicates a sprouting seed, a new beginning. For the seed to begin there has to be an end. Again, Mars provides the courage and fortitude to help face this difficult time. Aries is also an extremely spiritual sign; its ability to move into new dimensions is invaluable to Revati.

Symbol
FISH

Vishnu, one of the holy trinity of the Vedic gods, appeared in the form of a fish. He is known as Matsaya Avatar or the fish god. Fish is the most auspicious symbol. In the Vedic myths, gods come to earth as avatars or messengers to help humanity when a crisis was taking place. Vishnu came as the fish god to save humanity and aid with procreation. Fish has another important symbolism. It can only live in water; therefore Revati can only find true happiness when it immerses its soul in the ocean of infinity.

Ruling deities

Revati's ruling deity is Pushan, which is connected to the divisions of the solar year into two parts. When the Sun enters the nakshatra of Uttara Ashadha (around 15 January), it is considered to be the dawn of the year. This is the death and rebirth of the Sun. Pushan and Revati are both connected to transformation – the end of one journey and the beginning of another.

REVATI AIM IS FOR MOKSHA

Moksha or the need for self-realization is intense for Revati. Revati want to merge into the infinity and become one with its source. They want to let go of the individual ego and become 'mukta' or a person who has found the absolute – the divine light shines through them.

GUNA TRIPLICITY: SATTVA, SATTVA AND SATTVA

Sattva on all three levels shows Revati is ready for its goal of enlightenment. There is purity of thought, purpose and feeling. There is a great sense of peace and harmony and Revati are attuned to the laws of nature.

AYURVEDIC DOSHA IS KAPHA

Kapha are philosophical, calm and contented. They will work patiently through great trials and tribulations. Revati's being kapha further emphasizes its desire and goal for harmony. Revati will stay calm in crises.

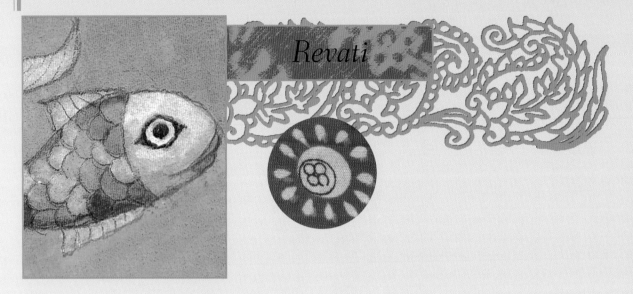

Revati

CHARACTERISTICS/ PERSONALITY TRAITS

Revati are the compassionate, caring and sensitive human beings of this Earth. They are the people whose kindness we take advantage of and whose good deeds we take for granted. When was the last time you appreciated or thanked your Revati friend? We are so used to their kindness that we forget to tell them how much we appreciate them. It is like living in paradise; after a time we begin to take the stunning surroundings of the place for granted. It can take an outsider to appreciate its wonderful beauty.

Revati may be the faceless workers that make the world a better place to live in and others remain blissfully ignorant of their service. Whether they are doctors or domestics, cleaners or computer operators, Revati work silently to keep the heart of the world running.

Revati get very disillusioned with those around them. They must remember that it is their personal choice to give of themselves unconditionally; they should not expect people to be grateful or admiring. Revati will only find pleasure in their selflessness if they act without making conditions.

They may lack self-confidence and feel that others do not appreciate their qualities. Revati are often very beautiful. They can have a tendency to allow themselves to become victims or perceive themselves as such.

HOW IT LINKS WITH THE WESTERN SUN SIGN AND RULER

Revati in Aries: Aries have the ability to sacrifice themselves so that others can live comfortably; this impulse is at its strongest in Revati. The Mars/Mercury combination gives both intellectual and physical strength to venture into the unknown, make extreme sacrifices and gestate the seed for future growth.

SPIRITUAL LIFE PATH

Revati's spiritual path is linked to sacrifice. The sacrifice is always connected to giving up what they desire for the good of others. Revati do that through service to humanity, often working in jobs that receive little appreciation or reward.

HOW REVATI RELATES TO OTHER NAKSHATRAS

Most compatible: Uttara Bhadra is the best relationship for Revati. Uttara Bhadra and Revati are spiritually connected. They need a deeper fulfilment from relationships than purely materialistic gains bring. Their connection will be strong and loving. Revati can be the answer to Purva Ashadha's restlessness; together they can find true peace.

Least compatible: Vishakha are the most difficult partners for Revati. Revati can become easily disillusioned and Vishakha may let Revati down. Revati must stop expecting Vishakha to be super-human and Vishakha should be generous towards Revati's fantasies.

Ideal sexual partner: The female elephant, Revati, is passionate towards the male elephant, Bharani. Revati and Bharani may fall madly in lust with each other, but this relationship can survive beyond the initial burst of passion as they are also compatible in other areas of life.

Unsuitable sexual partners: Dhanishta and Purva Bhadra, the lions, are sexually incompatible with Revati. Revati are gentle and spiritual, but have deep sexual needs. With Dhanishta and Purva Bhadra, there will be too much sexual rivalry and competitiveness, each unable to fulfil the other's desire.

For complete relationship information, see pages 128–139.

CUSPS

Those born at the end or beginning of the Shatabhishak should check the cusp details on page 143.

RELATIONSHIPS

Revati are the givers of the zodiac. They must try to appreciate the difference between positive giving and pouring their strength and energy into an endless pit from where there will be no spiritual or material returns.

In a relationship, Revati should look for a partner who really understands their spirituality and inner needs. Purely sexual relationships will be like a slow death for Revati. They must learn to have faith in themselves as they sometimes feel unloved and insecure; it can make them jealous of their partners. They must learn to trust. This is one of their greatest problems in relationships.

SEXUAL ENERGY LINKED TO THE FEMALE ELEPHANT

Revati have a strong and healthy sexual life. The female elephant suggest the passivity of Revati. They will rarely go out seeking for a partner.

They are not interested in purely sexual relationships. They want romance and social interaction to accompany it. In fact they can get easily bored or disinterested in the sexual aspect of relationships. Revati should be careful not to get involved with partners who are emotionally insensitive.

FAMOUS REVATI

Marlon Brando, Bette Davis, Billie Holliday, Omar Sharif.

Relationships

![mandala decoration] **THE PERFECT RELATIONSHIP FOR YOU**
Everyone can find a relationship that works for them. Whatever you need from a relationship, there is someone out there who can fulfil your needs. For each nakshatra there is an ideal relationship, but there are also several others that may not work. The trick to finding your best relationship is to look beyond mere physical attraction. The nakshatra compatibility will give you a comprehensive guide to relating to other nakshatras so that you can make informed choices about them.

RELATIONSHIPS IN INDIAN ASTROLOGY

Indian astrology believes that for a relationship to work well, it needs to be compatible on many levels – sexual, spiritual and emotional. The nakshatras give clues to every aspect of compatibility between a couple. There is a complicated number system by which relationships are assessed. In the West, people seldom look at the birth sign of the person they are falling in love with. Compatibility is usually looked at in later stages of the relationship. In India, there is more emphasis on examining compatibility before making a commitment. To be in a good relationship is meant to be a divine expression of love. For this to succeed, there has to be a correct understanding of the diverse factors that go into making relationships work.

SPECIAL ASPECTS OF INDIAN RELATIONSHIPS
Arranged Marriages

Traditionally in India parents arranged marriages for their children. One of the most important factors in trying to ensure that marriages were successful was comparing the birth charts of a couple to be matched to discover their true compatibility. Only after the astrologers had agreed to their astrological compatibility did a marriage go ahead.

Relationships in Mind, Body and Spirit

Relationships and marriages are considered to be a meeting of the mind, body and spirit. A marriage is seen as a rebirth – where two individual personalities merge into one. The relationship then has a life of its own; two souls are tied together in a spiritual connection.

A Punjabi bride preparing for her wedding day. She is seen wearing the traditional clothes and jewellery.

Karma and Relationships

Why are we attracted to someone we have never met before? What is the attraction? Indian philosophy believes that the partner of your life is part of your karma. Their good or bad qualities are part of your own learning process. We relate to and marry people with whom we have unfinished karma.

Relationships are for Life

Indian philosophy suggests that once you make a commitment, it is for life. It is the responsibility of the couple to face the ups and downs of life together. No one has complete perfection in a relationship. Aiming for that can create great unhappiness. We are all human with human failings and understanding this helps in maintaining good relationships.

The System of Relationship Compatibility

The method of Vedic compatibility is called the 'kuta' or units of agreement. It evaluates all the aspects of a relationship, such as love, attraction, sexual orientation, friendship, life direction, spiritual, times of life, etc. These are the important areas of compatibility we will be looking at:

1 **Friendships**
2 **Nakshatra support system**
3 **Nature: gods, humans and demons**
4 **Sexual: sex, attraction and love**
5 **Spiritual: connecting the prana or life force**
6 **Karmic connections**
7 **Total compatibility:** this synthesizes areas 1 to 6 and gives an indication of how the nakshatras will interact.

1 FRIENDSHIPS BETWEEN TWO NAKSHATRAS

The friendship between your nakshatra and your partner's nakshatra determines whether you and your partner will enjoy companionship, camaraderie, and mutual understanding, in the long run.

Planets relate to each other in a similar way to humans. They can feel friendly or inimical towards each other. If their feelings are mixed, then the relationship is known as neutral. This relationship is expressed by the nakshatras through their rulerships. For example, Ketu rules Ashwini nakshatra, so Ashwini will have full relationship compatibility with Pushya, as Pushya's ruler, Saturn, is a friend of Ketu.

THE NAKSHATRAS RULERSHIPS

Ketu	Magha, Mula and Ashwini
Venus	Purva Phalguni, Purva Ashadha and Bharani
Sun	Uttara Phalguni, Uttara Ashadha and Krittika
Moon	Hasta, Shravana and Rohini
Mars	Mrigasira, Chitra and Dhanishta
Rahu	Ardra, Swati and Shatabhishak
Jupiter	Punarvasu, Vishakha and Purva Bhadra
Saturn	Pushya, Anuradha and Uttara Bhadra
Mercury	Ashlesha, Jyeshta and Revati

NATURAL PLANETARY RELATIONSHIPS

PLANET	FRIENDS	NEUTRALS	ENEMIES
THE SUN	Moon, Mars	Mercury Jupiter	Venus, Saturn
MOON	Sun, Mercury	Mars, Jupiter	Venus, Saturn
MARS	Sun, Moon Jupiter	Venus, Saturn	Mercury
MERCURY	Sun, Venus	Mars, Jupiter Saturn	Moon
JUPITER	Sun, Moon, Mars	Saturn	Mercury, Venus
VENUS	Mercury, Saturn	Mars, Jupiter	Sun, Moon
SATURN	Venus, Mercury	Jupiter	Sun, Moon, Mars
RAHU AND KETU	Mercury, Venus Saturn	Mars	Sun, Moon, Jupiter

Some planets are friendly with others but others do not return their feelings. The Moon is friendly to Mercury, but Mercury does not like the Moon at all. Therefore, if your nakshatra is Ashlesha, ruled by the Moon, and you are in love with Rohini, ruled by Mercury, you may find your feelings are not reciprocated.

2   THE NAKSHATRAS' SUPPORT SYSTEM

The nakshatras have a unique way of interrelating with each other. This system is known as the Tara Bala. 'Tara' is another name for the nakshatras and 'Bala' means 'strength'. Together, it means the strength your natal nakshatra can derive from other nakshatras.

This is a very important way of understanding how the nakshatras support each other. At times, due to the position of your partner's nakshatra from your natal nakshatra, the relationship can override other planetary indications and give positive results, even if the planets are mutually inimical to each other.

Henna is used to ceremonially decorate the hands of this Hindu bride for her wedding day.

Personalized Tara Bala Chart

		1st Cycle	2nd Cycle	3rd Cycle
1	Similar	MAGHA	MuLA	Ashwini
2	Good for business	PuRVA Phalguni	PuRVA Ashadha	BHARANi
3	Difficult	UTTARA Phalguni	uttara Ashadha	KRittika
4	Happy	HASTA	ShRAVANA	Rohini
5	Obstructive	Chitra	DhANishtA	MRigaSira
6	Spiritual	Swati	ShAtAbhishAk Penny	ArdRa DIANE
7	Complex	VishaKha	PuRVA Bhadra	PuNARVASu
8	Good	AnuRAdha	UttARA Bhadra	Pushya
9	Best	Jyeshta	Revati	Ashlesha

Write your own natal Sun nakshatra opposite Similar (under 1st cycle), then write the other nakshatras in the vertical column until you reach the ninth one from your own. Put the tenth nakshatra from your birth Sun at the top of the second column (2nd cycle), then write the others vertically till you reach the 18th nakshatra from your own. Finally, put the 19th nakshatra from your birth Sun at the top of the third column (3rd cycle), then write the others vertically till you reach the 27th nakshatra from your own.

The planetary strength you derive from each nakshatra is shown below. This grid will be different for individual nakshatras.

1 Similar: The other nakshatras in this row are ruled by the same planet and are very similar to you. Relationships between these nakshatras give average strength to each other. They will be good friends, but may not want to make a long-term commitment to you.

2 Good for business: These nakshatras create wealth and prosperity for you. You can have profitable relationships with them. A practical relationship based on business or mutual interests will be beneficial.

3 Difficult: These nakshatras are full of challenges for you. They are not able to give you the support you want.

4 Happy: These nakshatras bring warmth and happiness to your relationship. They will be a positive strength to you.

5 Obstructive: These nakshatras impede your personal growth. There can be rivalry and competitiveness. They are not supportive of you.

6 Spiritual: These relationships will lead to the realization of ambitions – both spiritual and material. They will give great strength to you.

7 Complex: These nakshatras bring out the negative qualities in you. They do not offer you any kind of support. You may get involved in a complicated relationship with them which has the potential to make you unhappy.

8 Good: These nakshatras bring immeasurable support and strength to relationships with you. These relationships have the capacity to override all types of difficulty.

9 Best: These nakshatras are considered excellent relationships for you. There should be mutual love, support and friendship.

3 THE TEMPERAMENTAL COMPATIBILITY: GODS, HUMANS, AND DEMONS

Nakshatras are classified into three groups: gods, humans and demons. Gods reflect the guna of Sattva, humans of Rajas, and demons of Tamas. The gods are steady; humans dynamic; demons sluggish. These qualities are usually said to reflect the nature of an individual. For people to be truly compatible, they should choose a partner who has a similar personality to them – gods must relate to gods, humans to humans, and demons to demons.

In today's environment where no one follows rigid rules, these classifications are not necessarily valid, but they do explain the temperament of your partner.

GODS (SATTVA)	HUMANS (RAJAS)	DEMONS (TAMAS)
Ashwini	Bharani	Krittika
Mrigasira	Rohini	Ashlesha
Punarvasu	Ardra	Magha
Pushya	Purva Phalguni	Chitra
Hasta	Uttara Phalguni	Vishakha
Swati	Purva Ashadha	Jyeshta
Anuradha	Uttara Ashadha	Mula
Shravana	Purva Bhadra	Dhanishta
Revati	Uttara Bhadra	Shatabhishak

4 SEXUAL COMPATIBILITY

Sexual compatibility represents the physical attraction and love between partners. This is linked to the animal signs of the nakshatras. The animal signs show the evolution of an individual. Animals that are hostile to each other in the animal kingdom will not have a good sexual compatibility. It is important to remember that sexual compatibility does not necessarily mean that you are in harmony in the other areas of a relationship.

ANIMAL SEXUALITY	MALE	FEMALE
Horse	Ashwini	Shatabhishak
Elephant	Bharani	Revati
Sheep	Pushya	Krittika
Serpent	Rohini	Mrigasira
Dog	Mula	Ardra
Cat	Ashlesha	Punarvasu
Rat	Magha	Purva Phalguni
Cow	Uttara Phalguni	Uttara Bhadra
Buffalo	Swati	Hasta
Tiger	Vishakha	Chitra
Deer	Jyeshta	Anuradha
Monkey	Purva Ashadha	Shravana
Lion	Purva Bhadra	Dhanishta
Mongoose	Uttara Ashadha	

SEXUAL ANTAGONISTS

The sexual relationships of the following pairs do not work.

1 Cow (Uttara Phalguni and Uttara Bhadra) with **Tiger** (Vishakha and Chitra)

2 Horse (Ashwini and Shatabhishak) with **Buffalo** (Swati and Hasta)

3 Dog (Mula and Ardra) with **Deer** (Jyeshta and Anuradha)

4 Serpent (Rohini and Mrigasira) with **Mongoose** (Uttara Ashada)

5 Monkey (Purva Ashada and Shravana) with **Sheep** (Pushya and Krittika)

6 Cat (Ashlesha and Punarvasu) with **Rat** (Magha and Purva Phalguni)

5 SPIRITUAL COMPATIBILITY

Spiritual compatibility is very important for true compatibility. This takes into account the doshas (body types): vata, pitta, and kapha. Each nakshatra is classified as a specific body type. The doshas are studied to understand the interplay of your subtle body. The subtle body plays an important part in connecting souls on a deeper level. This shows how the prana or life force is flowing within us. This is one of the most important connections for successful relationships.

The doshas reflect the temperaments and attitudes, as well as the ability to spiritually connect. The doshas of the two partners help in birth of children. For the pranic (astral) body to connect, it is important that your nakshatra dosha should be different from your partner. If two partners have similar doshas, they are unable to create harmony with their spirit body.

VATA	PITTA	KAPHA
Ashwini	Bharani	Krittika
Ardra	Mrigasira	Rohini
Punarvasu	Pushya	Ashlesha
Uttara Phalguni	Purva Phalguni	Magha
Hasta	Chitra	Swati
Jyeshta	Anuradha	Vishakha
Mula	Purva Ashadha	Uttara Ashadha
Shatabhishak	Dhanishta	Shravana
Purva Bhadra	Uttara Bhadra	Revati

SOME RELATIONSHIPS ARE SPIRITUALLY COMPLEX

Some nakshatras have complex relationships with others. They may have good points in all other compatibility, but in reality they have to face some karmic restrictions that can create unhappiness.

Ashwini and Jyeshta
Bharani and Anuradha
Krittika and Vishakha
Rohini and Swati
Ardra and Shravana
Punarvasu and Uttara Ashadha
Pushya and Purva Ashada
Ashlesha and Mula
Magha and Revati
Purva Phalguni and Uttara Bhadra
Uttara Phalguni and Purva Bhadra
Hasta and Shatabhishak
Mrigasira and Dhanishta

6 KARMIC RELATIONSHIPS

Rahu and Ketu indicate intense karmic relationships. If you are involved with any of the Rahu or Ketu nakshatras, the relationship will have an added shadowy quality. There will be a feeling that there are some greater issues being worked out than is immediately obvious. Sometimes emotions can be churned up greatly in order to find the essence of the relationship. Although all relationships are karmic, these relationships have a greater depth and fervour. Rahu and Ketu nakshatras who connect with each other may feel they have found their soulmates, but at the same time they experience challenging situations in life that can bring emotional upheavals.
Rahu nakshatras:
Ardra, Swati and Shatabhishak
Ketu nakshatras:
Ashwini, Magha and Mula

THE TOTAL NAKSHATRA COMPATIBILITY

The nakshatras at birth give us clear instruction as to what tools are available for us in this life. The nakshatras, their strengths and weaknesses, their inner and outer natures, provide clues to our own instinct and how we will use this while interacting with others. Nakshatra compatibility is a complex way of looking at relationships. You may be very compatible in one area of relationship, e.g. sexually, but if other areas are not compatible, you may not get total compatibility. The nakshatra compatibility grid takes into account all the negative and positive forces affecting nakshatra relationships and synthesizes it in a simple-to-use format.

Nakshatra Compatibility Grid

0–25 BELOW AVERAGE; 25–50 AVERAGE; 50–75 GOOD; 75–100 GREAT

	Ashw	Bha	Kri	Roh	Mri	Ard	Pun	Pus	Ashl	Ma	PP	UP
Ashw	77	91	61	62	61	44	55	83	75	55	67	34
Bha	91	77	65	64	43	69	76	61	66	53	47	60
Kri	61	65	65	30	54	49	56	68	57	47	43	53
Roh	62	64	30	55	77	64	66	75	33	28	66	72
Mri	61	43	54	77	64	78	67	41	47	57	46	73
Ard	44	69	49	64	78	77	51	55	33	58	75	61
Pun	55	76	56	66	67	51	57	76	60	51	62	50
Pus	83	61	68	75	41	55	76	77	80	50	39	52
Ashl	75	66	57	33	47	33	60	80	77	41	41	50
Ma	55	53	47	28	57	58	51	50	41	77	83	55
PP	67	47	43	66	46	75	62	39	41	83	77	80
UP	34	60	53	72	73	61	50	52	50	55	80	61
Has	27	50	44	69	82	67	57	69	53	39	55	58
Chi	47	22	61	49	37	65	58	30	67	58	19	47
Swa	70	78	32	42	50	75	74	69	30	27	66	69
Vis	55	50	51	30	50	46	51	54	41	54	55	50
An	66	47	60	80	47	53	62	47	53	66	61	80
Jye	36	53	76	67	53	14	22	55	69	88	66	39
Mul	33	53	65	36	51	42	29	47	61	66	53	32
PA	66	47	47	53	40	77	65	33	42	53	50	75
UA	66	72	30	37	55	67	58	63	27	15	60	68
Shr	72	77	32	50	39	61	68	75	36	11	50	61
Dha	53	26	70	53	35	50	46	24	60	55	19	40
Sha	38	53	75	76	65	33	25	36	50	66	50	37
PB	42	62	54	60	69	48	41	60	39	47	64	39
UB	64	11	50	75	49	72	70	50	55	50	44	75
Rev	72	69	32	53	74	72	69	72	33	33	67	69

HOW TO STUDY THE NAKSHATRA COMPATIBILITY CHART

Look in the vertical column for your nakshatra and the horizontal column for your partner's nakshatra. The number you arrive at is the percentage compatibility you have with your partner. For example, if your nakshatra is Chitra and your partner's is Shatabhishak, you find Chitra in the vertical column and Shatabhishak in the horizontal one. You will see the number is 69. Therefore your compatibility with your partner is 69 per cent.

i	Swa	Vis	An	Jye	Mul	PA	UA	Shr	Dha	Sha	PB	UB	Rev
	70	55	66	36	33	66	66	72	53	38	42	64	72
	78	50	47	53	53	47	72	77	26	53	62	11	69
	32	51	60	76	65	47	30	32	70	75	54	50	32
	42	30	80	67	36	53	37	50	53	76	60	75	53
	50	50	47	53	51	40	55	39	35	65	69	49	74
	75	46	53	14	42	77	67	61	50	33	48	72	72
	74	51	62	22	29	65	58	68	46	25	41	70	69
	69	54	47	55	47	33	63	75	24	36	60	50	72
	30	41	53	69	61	42	27	36	60	50	39	55	33
	27	54	66	88	66	53	15	11	55	66	47	50	33
	66	55	61	66	53	50	60	50	19	50	64	44	67
	69	50	80	39	32	75	68	61	40	37	39	75	69
	72	53	72	36	42	75	64	66	51	27	38	72	66
	65	74	23	62	75	36	55	58	50	69	45	18	43
	77	40	58	41	63	75	55	61	65	61	60	53	24
	40	60	59	72	66	38	32	36	70	70	49	41	18
	58	59	77	86	41	36	64	72	32	61	66	47	72
	41	72	86	77	39	44	50	55	68	47	26	55	55
	63	66	41	39	77	77	36	39	65	58	41	66	72
	75	38	36	44	77	77	77	61	26	64	66	61	83
	55	32	64	50	36	77	68	58	52	63	66	83	55
	61	36	72	55	39	61	58	77	61	47	66	80	64
	65	70	32	68	65	26	52	61	63	77	58	17	36
	61	70	61	47	58	64	63	47	77	77	51	66	42
	60	49	66	26	41	66	66	66	58	51	60	76	68
	53	41	47	55	66	61	83	80	17	66	76	77	91
	24	18	72	55	72	83	55	64	36	42	68	91	77

Sexual Compatibility Grid

0 = NONE; 25 BELOW AVERAGE; 50 AVERAGE; 75 GOOD; 100 PERFECT

	Ashw	Bha	Kri	Roh	Mri	Ard	Pun	Pus	Ashl	Ma	PP	UP
Ashw	100	50	50	75	75	50	50	50	50	50	50	25
Bha	50	100	75	75	75	50	50	75	50	50	50	25
Kri	50	75	100	50	50	25	50	100	50	25	25	75
Roh	75	75	50	100	100	50	25	50	25	25	25	25
Mri	75	75	50	100	100	50	25	50	25	25	25	25
Ard	50	50	25	50	50	100	50	25	50	25	25	50
Pun	50	50	50	25	25	50	100	50	100	0	0	50
Pus	50	75	100	50	50	25	50	100	50	25	25	75
Ashl	50	50	50	25	25	50	100	50	100	0	0	50
Ma	50	50	25	25	25	25	0	25	0	100	100	50
PP	50	50	25	25	25	25	0	25	0	100	100	50
UP	25	25	75	25	25	50	50	75	50	50	50	100
Has	0	75	75	25	25	50	50	75	50	50	50	75
Chi	25	25	25	50	50	25	25	25	25	50	50	0
Swa	0	75	75	25	25	50	50	75	50	50	50	75
Vis	25	25	25	50	50	25	25	25	25	50	50	0
An	75	50	50	50	50	0	75	50	75	50	50	75
Jye	75	50	50	50	50	0	75	50	75	50	50	75
Mul	50	50	25	50	50	100	50	25	50	25	25	50
PA	75	75	0	50	50	50	75	0	75	50	50	50
UA	50	50	75	0	0	25	50	75	50	25	25	50
Shr	75	75	0	50	50	50	75	0	75	50	50	50
Dha	25	0	25	50	50	25	25	25	25	50	50	25
Sha	100	50	50	75	75	50	50	50	50	50	50	25
PB	25	0	25	50	50	25	25	25	25	50	50	25
UB	25	50	75	25	25	50	50	75	50	50	50	100
Rev	50	100	75	75	75	50	50	75	50	50	50	25

HOW TO STUDY THE SEXUAL COMPATIBILITY CHART

Look in the vertical column for your nakshatra and the horizontal column for your partner's nakshatra. The number you arrive at is the percentage sexual compatibility you have with your partner. For example, if your nakshatra is Magha and your partner's is Ashwini, you find Magha in the vertical column and Ashwini in the horizontal one. You will see the number is 50. Therefore your sexual compatibility with your partner is 50 per cent.

hi	Swa	Vis	An	Jye	Mul	PA	UA	Shr	Dha	Sha	PB	UB	Rev
	0	25	75	75	50	75	50	75	25	100	25	25	50
	75	25	50	50	50	75	50	75	0	50	0	25	100
	75	25	50	50	25	0	75	0	25	50	25	75	75
	25	50	50	50	50	50	0	50	50	75	50	25	75
	25	50	50	50	50	50	0	50	50	75	50	25	75
	50	25	0	0	100	50	25	50	25	50	25	50	50
	50	25	75	75	50	75	50	75	25	50	25	50	50
	75	25	50	50	25	0	75	0	25	50	25	75	75
	50	25	75	75	50	75	50	75	25	50	25	50	50
	50	50	50	50	25	50	25	50	50	50	50	50	50
	50	50	50	50	25	50	25	50	50	50	50	50	50
	75	0	75	75	50	50	50	50	25	25	25	100	25
	100	25	50	50	50	50	50	50	25	0	25	75	75
	25	100	25	25	25	25	50	25	25	25	25	0	25
	100	25	50	50	50	50	50	50	25	0	25	75	75
	25	100	25	25	25	25	50	25	25	25	25	0	25
	50	25	100	100	0	50	50	50	25	75	25	75	50
	50	25	100	100	0	50	50	50	25	75	25	75	50
	50	25	0	0	100	50	25	50	25	50	25	50	50
	50	25	50	50	50	100	75	100	50	75	50	50	75
	50	50	50	50	25	75	100	75	50	50	50	50	50
	50	25	50	50	50	100	50	100	50	75	50	50	75
	25	25	25	25	25	50	50	50	100	25	100	25	0
	0	25	75	75	50	75	50	75	25	100	25	25	50
	25	25	25	25	25	50	50	50	100	25	100	25	0
	75	0	75	75	50	50	50	50	25	25	25	100	50
	75	25	50	50	50	75	50	75	0	50	0	25	100

8 | RELATIONSHIPS

Spiritual Compatibility Grid

A RED DOT SHOWS NO SPIRITUAL COMPATIBILITY; A BLUE DOT SHOWS 100 PER CENT COMPATIBILITY

	Ashw	Bha	Kri	Roh	Mri	Ard	Pun	Pus	Ashl	Ma	PP	UP
Ashw	●	●	●	●	●	●	●	●	●	●	●	●
Bha	●	●	●	●	●	●	●	●	●	●	●	●
Kri	●	●	●	●	●	●	●	●	●	●	●	●
Roh	●	●	●	●	●	●	●	●	●	●	●	●
Mri	●	●	●	●	●	●	●	●	●	●	●	●
Ard	●	●	●	●	●	●	●	●	●	●	●	●
Pun	●	●	●	●	●	●	●	●	●	●	●	●
Pus	●	●	●	●	●	●	●	●	●	●	●	●
Ashl	●	●	●	●	●	●	●	●	●	●	●	●
Ma	●	●	●	●	●	●	●	●	●	●	●	●
PP	●	●	●	●	●	●	●	●	●	●	●	●
UP	●	●	●	●	●	●	●	●	●	●	●	●
Has	●	●	●	●	●	●	●	●	●	●	●	●
Chi	●	●	●	●	●	●	●	●	●	●	●	●
Swa	●	●	●	●	●	●	●	●	●	●	●	●
Vis	●	●	●	●	●	●	●	●	●	●	●	●
An	●	●	●	●	●	●	●	●	●	●	●	●
Jye	●	●	●	●	●	●	●	●	●	●	●	●
Mul	●	●	●	●	●	●	●	●	●	●	●	●
PA	●	●	●	●	●	●	●	●	●	●	●	●
UA	●	●	●	●	●	●	●	●	●	●	●	●
Shr	●	●	●	●	●	●	●	●	●	●	●	●
Dha	●	●	●	●	●	●	●	●	●	●	●	●
Sha	●	●	●	●	●	●	●	●	●	●	●	●
PB	●	●	●	●	●	●	●	●	●	●	●	●
UB	●	●	●	●	●	●	●	●	●	●	●	●
Rev	●	●	●	●	●	●	●	●	●	●	●	●

HOW TO STUDY THE SPIRITUAL COMPATIBILITY CHART

Look in the vertical column for your nakshatra and the horizontal column for your partner's nakshatra. If there is a red dot, there is no spiritual compatibility; if there is a blue dot, it indicates 100 per cent spiritual compatibility. For example, if your nakshatra is Ashlesha and your partners is Uttara Bhadra, you find Ashlesha in the vertical column and Uttara Bhadra from the horizontal one, there is a blue dot in that space. Therefore your spiritual compatibility with your partner is 100 per cent.

Perry & I have 100% spiritually compatibility

i	Swa	Vis	An	Jye	Mul	PA	UA	Shr	Dha	Sha	PB	UB	Rev
	●	●	●	●	●	●	●	●	●	●	●	●	●
	●	●	●	●	●	●	●	●	●	●	●	●	●
	●	●	●	●	●	●	●	●	●	●	●	●	●
	●	●	●	●	●	●	●	●	●	●	●	●	●
	●	●	●	●	●	●	●	●	●	●	●	●	●
	●	●	●	●	●	●	●	●	●	●	●	●	●
	●	●	●	●	●	●	●	●	●	●	●	●	●
	●	●	●	●	●	●	●	●	●	●	●	●	●
	●	●	●	●	●	●	●	●	●	●	●	●	●
	●	●	●	●	●	●	●	●	●	(●)	●	●	●
	●	●	●	●	●	●	●	●	●	●	●	●	●
	●	●	●	●	●	●	●	●	●	●	●	●	●
	●	●	●	●	●	●	●	●	●	●	●	●	●
	●	●	●	●	●	●	●	●	●	●	●	●	●
	●	●	●	●	●	●	●	●	●	●	●	●	●
	●	●	●	●	●	●	●	●	●	●	●	●	●
	●	●	●	●	●	●	●	●	●	●	●	●	●
	●	●	●	●	●	●	●	●	●	●	●	●	●
	●	●	●	●	●	●	●	●	●	●	●	●	●
	●	●	●	●	●	●	●	●	●	●	●	●	●
	●	●	●	●	●	●	●	●	●	●	●	●	●
	●	●	●	●	●	●	●	●	●	●	●	●	●
	●	●	●	●	●	●	●	●	●	●	●	●	●
	●	●	●	●	●	●	●	●	●	●	●	●	●

ASHWINI

Year	Date	Time
1940	13	02:37
1941	13	08:54
1942	13	15:06
1943	13	21:11
1944	13	03:19
1945	13	09:30
1946	13	15:40
1947	13	21:44
1948	13	03:49
1949	13	10:01
1950	13	16:13
1951	13	22:19
1952	13	04:32
1953	13	10:47
1954	13	16:56
1955	13	23:00
1956	13	05:06
1957	13	11:18
1958	13	17:30
1959	13	23:33
1960	13	05:40
1961	13	11:52
1962	13	18:01
1963	14	00:10
1964	13	06:22
1965	13	12:36
1966	13	18:49
1967	14	00:53
1968	13	06:58
1969	13	13:13
1970	13	19:19
1971	14	01:22
1972	13	07:31
1973	13	13:38
1974	13	19:54
1975	14	02:02
1976	13	08:12
1977	13	14:31
1978	13	20:37
1979	14	02:41
1980	13	08:51
1981	13	14:59
1982	13	21:12
1983	14	03:17
1984	13	09:19
1985	13	15:35
1986	13	21:42
1987	14	03:48
1988	13	10:04
1989	13	16:15
1990	13	22:27
1991	14	04:34
1992	13	10:37
1993	13	16:55
1994	13	23:01
1995	14	05:01
1996	13	11:14
1997	13	17:21
1998	13	23:34
1999	14	05:47
2000	13	11:52
2001	13	18:12
2002	14	00:18
2003	14	06:17
2004	13	12:32
2005	13	18:39
2006	14	00:49
2007	14	06:58
2008	13	12:59
2009	13	19:17
2010	14	01:26

BHARANI

Year	Date	Time
1940	26	18:33
1941	27	00:45
1942	27	06:55
1943	27	13:08
1944	26	19:08
1945	27	01:23
1946	27	07:36
1947	27	13:31
1948	26	19:45
1949	27	01:55
1950	27	08:00
1951	27	14:15
1952	26	20:21
1953	27	02:37
1954	27	08:53
1955	27	14:47
1956	26	21:00
1957	27	03:13
1958	27	09:16
1959	27	15:29
1960	26	21:31
1961	27	03:42
1962	27	09:57
1963	27	15:56
1964	26	22:13
1965	27	04:31
1966	27	10:34
1967	27	16:47
1968	26	22:51
1969	27	05:01
1970	27	11:15
1971	27	17:10
1972	26	23:21
1973	27	05:35
1974	27	11:38
1975	27	17:53
1976	27	00:04
1977	27	06:17
1978	27	12:33
1979	27	18:30
1980	27	00:40
1981	27	06:56
1982	27	13:20
1983	27	19:08
1984	27	01:16
1985	27	07:21
1986	27	13:36
1987	27	19:38
1988	27	01:50
1989	27	08:11
1990	27	14:14
1991	27	20:23
1992	27	02:33
1993	27	08:40
1994	27	14:54
1995	27	20:53
1996	27	03:00
1997	27	09:17
1998	27	15:21
1999	27	21:32
2000	27	03:47
2001	27	09:58
2002	27	16:09
2003	27	22:10
2004	27	04:17
2005	27	10:33
2006	27	16:38
2007	27	22:44
2008	27	04:55
2009	27	11:04
2010	27	17:14

KRITTIKA

Year	Date	Time
1940	10	12:40
1941	10	18:58
1942	11	01:10
1943	11	07:14
1944	10	13:24
1945	10	19:37
1946	11	01:44
1947	11	07:48
1948	10	13:56
1949	10	20:08
1950	11	02:17
1951	11	08:21
1952	10	14:34
1953	10	20:51
1954	11	02:59
1955	11	09:04
1956	10	15:12
1957	10	21:23
1958	11	03:32
1959	11	09:36
1960	10	15:44
1961	10	21:59
1962	11	04:04
1963	11	10:10
1964	10	16:25
1965	10	22:38
1966	11	04:50
1967	11	10:56
1968	10	17:02
1969	10	23:17
1970	11	05:21
1971	11	11:24
1972	10	17:35
1973	10	23:42
1974	11	05:53
1975	11	12:02
1976	10	18:12
1977	11	00:33
1978	11	06:40
1979	11	12:42
1980	10	18:55
1981	11	01:03
1982	11	07:12
1983	11	13:19
1984	10	19:23
1985	11	01:38
1986	11	07:45
1987	11	13:46
1988	10	20:04
1989	11	02:16
1990	11	08:25
1991	11	14:35
1992	10	20:39
1993	11	02:56
1994	11	09:03
1995	11	15:01
1996	10	21:17
1997	11	03:24
1998	11	09:31
1999	11	15:44
2000	10	21:51
2001	11	04:11
2002	11	10:19
2003	11	16:16
2004	10	22:33
2005	11	04:41
2006	11	10:46
2007	11	16:58
2008	10	23:01
2009	11	05:16
2010	11	11:26

ROHINI

Year	Date	Time
1940	24	08.58
1941	24	15.14
1942	24	21.19
1943	25	03.33
1944	24	09.38
1945	24	15.51
1946	24	22.04
1947	25	03.59
1948	24	10.14
1949	24	16.27
1950	24	22.27
1951	25	04.40
1952	24	10.49
1953	24	17.03
1954	24	23.19
1955	25	05.15
1956	24	11.27
1957	24	17.43
1958	24	23.41
1959	25	05.54
1960	24	12.01
1961	24	18.10
1962	25	00.24
1963	25	06.22
1964	24	12.37
1965	24	18.58
1966	25	00.59
1967	25	07.11
1968	24	13.20
1969	24	19.28
1970	25	01.40
1971	25	07.37
1972	24	13.47
1973	24	20.03
1974	25	02.03
1975	25	08.15
1976	24	14.29
1977	24	20.41
1978	25	02.56
1979	25	08.57
1980	24	15.06
1981	24	21.24
1982	25	03.23
1983	25	09.31
1984	24	15.43
1985	24	21.48
1986	25	04.00
1987	25	10.01
1988	24	16.12
1989	24	22.34
1990	25	04.37
1991	25	10.45
1992	24	16.59
1993	24	23.06
1994	25	05.16
1995	25	11.19
1996	24	17.26
1997	24	23.43
1998	25	05.44
1999	25	11.52
2000	24	18.10
2001	25	00.21
2002	25	06.31
2003	25	12.34
2004	24	18.42
2005	25	00.57
2006	25	07.01
2007	25	13.05
2008	24	19.20
2009	25	01.28
2010	25	07.35

MRIGASIRA

Year	Date	Time
1940	7	06.50
1941	7	13.06
1942	7	19.17
1943	8	01.21
1944	7	07.34
1945	7	13.48
1946	7	19.53
1947	8	01.57
1948	7	08.08
1949	7	14.19
1950	7	20.26
1951	8	02.30
1952	7	08.42
1953	7	14.59
1954	7	21.06
1955	8	03.11
1956	7	09.23
1957	7	15.33
1958	7	21.39
1959	8	03.44
1960	7	09.53
1961	7	16.09
1962	7	22.12
1963	8	04.17
1964	7	10.33
1965	7	16.45
1966	7	22.55
1967	8	05.03
1968	7	11.11
1969	7	17.27
1970	7	23.29
1971	8	05.31
1972	7	11.45
1973	7	17.52
1974	7	23.59
1975	8	06.07
1976	7	12.18
1977	7	18.37
1978	8	00.45
1979	8	06.48
1980	7	13.05
1981	7	19.13
1982	8	01.17
1983	8	07.26
1984	7	13.32
1985	7	19.46
1986	8	01.51
1987	8	07.51
1988	7	14.10
1989	7	20.22
1990	8	02.28
1991	8	08.41
1992	7	14.47
1993	7	21.01
1994	8	03.09
1995	8	09.07
1996	7	15.25
1997	7	21.33
1998	8	03.35
1999	8	09.48
2000	7	15.57
2001	7	22.14
2002	8	04.24
2003	8	10.22
2004	7	16.40
2005	7	22.48
2006	8	04.49
2007	8	11.02
2008	7	17.08
2009	7	23.21
2010	8	05.30

ARDRA

Year	Date	Time
1940	21	05.54
1941	21	12.10
1942	21	18.12
1943	22	00.27
1944	21	06.36
1945	21	12.46
1946	21	19.00
1947	22	00.56
1948	21	07.10
1949	21	13.26
1950	21	19.22
1951	22	01.35
1952	21	07.46
1953	21	13.56
1954	21	20.12
1955	22	02.11
1956	21	08.24
1957	21	14.40
1958	21	20.36
1959	22	02.47
1960	21	08.59
1961	21	15.05
1962	21	21.18
1963	22	03.18
1964	21	09.31
1965	21	15.52
1966	21	21.52
1967	22	04.04
1968	21	10.18
1969	21	16.23
1970	21	22.34
1971	22	04.34
1972	21	10.43
1973	21	16.59
1974	21	22.57
1975	22	05.06
1976	21	11.24
1977	21	17.32
1978	21	23.47
1979	22	05.52
1980	21	12.02
1981	21	18.19
1982	22	00.17
1983	22	06.24
1984	21	12.39
1985	21	18.43
1986	22	00.52
1987	22	06.56

Year	Date	Time
1988	21	13.06
1989	21	19.26
1990	22	01.28
1991	22	07.36
1992	21	13.53
1993	21	19.59
1994	22	02.07
1995	22	08.13
1996	21	14.21
1997	21	20.37
1998	22	02.38
1999	22	08.44
2000	21	15.02
2001	21	21.12
2002	22	03.20
2003	22	09.28
2004	21	15.37
2005	21	21.50
2006	22	03.52
2007	22	09.57
2008	21	16.13
2009	21	22.21
2010	22	04.26

PUNARVASU

Year	Date	Time
1940	5	05.30
1941	5	11.42
1942	5	17.51
1943	5	23.57
1944	5	06.12
1945	5	12.25
1946	5	18.30
1947	6	00.36
1948	5	06.48
1949	5	12.57
1950	5	19.03
1951	6	01.08
1952	5	07.20
1953	5	13.35
1954	5	19.41
1955	6	01.48
1956	5	08.02
1957	5	14.11
1958	5	20.15
1959	6	02.22
1960	5	08.31
1961	5	14.45
1962	5	20.49
1963	6	02.54
1964	5	09.11
1965	5	15.21
1966	5	21.29
1967	6	03.39
1968	5	09.49
1969	5	16.03
1970	5	22.06
1971	6	04.08
1972	5	10.24
1973	5	16.30
1974	5	22.34
1975	6	04.44
1976	5	10.54
1977	5	17.10
1978	5	23.19
1979	6	05.24
1980	5	11.43
1981	5	17.50
1982	5	23.52
1983	6	06.03
1984	5	12.10
1985	5	18.21
1986	6	00.28
1987	6	06.28
1988	5	12.46
1989	5	18.57
1990	6	01.00
1991	6	07.15
1992	5	13.24
1993	5	19.36
1994	6	01.44
1995	6	07.44
1996	5	14.02
1997	5	20.11
1998	6	02.09
1999	6	08.24
2000	5	14.33
2001	5	20.45
2002	6	02.57
2003	6	08.58
2004	5	15.16
2005	5	21.25
2006	6	03.23
2007	6	09.37
2008	5	15.46
2009	5	21.54
2010	6	04.04

PUSHYA

Year	Date	Time
1940	19	05.04
1941	19	11.19
1942	19	17.17
1943	19	23.32
1944	19	05.46
1945	19	11.53
1946	19	18.07
1947	20	00.07
1948	19	06.20
1949	19	12.35
1950	19	18.31
1951	20	00.43
1952	19	06.56
1953	19	13.02
1954	19	19.17
1955	20	01.20
1956	19	07.32
1957	19	13.49
1958	19	19.44
1959	20	01.55
1960	19	08.09
1961	19	14.12
1962	19	20.25
1963	20	02.29
1964	19	08.40
1965	19	14.58
1966	19	20.57
1967	20	03.09
1968	19	09.27
1969	19	15.30
1970	19	21.40
1971	20	03.44
1972	19	09.52
1973	19	16.07
1974	19	22.05
1975	20	04.13
1976	19	10.32
1977	19	16.37
1978	19	22.49
1979	20	04.59
1980	19	11.10
1981	19	17.26
1982	19	23.25
1983	20	05.31
1984	19	11.48
1985	19	17.51
1986	19	23.59
1987	20	06.06
1988	19	12.14
1989	19	18.30
1990	20	00.33
1991	20	06.42
1992	19	13.01
1993	19	19.06
1994	20	01.13
1995	20	07.22
1996	19	13.30
1997	19	19.43
1998	20	01.45
1999	20	07.51
2000	19	14.09
2001	19	20.16
2002	20	02.23
2003	20	08.35
2004	19	14.45
2005	19	20.56
2006	20	02.59
2007	20	09.04
2008	19	15.20
2009	19	21.27
2010	20	03.31

ASHLESHA

Year	Date	Time
1940	2	03.59
1941	2	10.07
1942	2	16.14
1943	2	22.22
1944	2	04.37
1945	2	10.50
1946	2	16.54
1947	2	23.02
1948	2	05.16
1949	2	11.23
1950	2	17.28
1951	2	23.36
1952	2	05.47
1953	2	11.59
1954	2	18.05
1955	3	00.13
1956	2	06.29
1957	2	12.37
1958	2	18.40
1959	3	00.49
1960	2	06.58
1961	2	13.10
1962	2	19.15
1963	3	01.21
1964	2	07.38
1965	2	13.46
1966	2	19.51
1967	3	02.04
1968	2	08.15
1969	2	14.27
1970	2	20.32
1971	3	02.36
1972	2	08.51
1973	2	14.56
1974	2	20.58
1975	3	03.11
1976	2	09.20
1977	2	15.32
1978	2	21.41
1979	3	03.48
1980	2	10.08
1981	2	16.16
1982	2	22.17
1983	3	04.30
1984	2	10.38
1985	2	16.45
1986	2	22.54
1987	3	04.56
1988	2	11.12
1989	2	17.21
1990	2	23.22
1991	3	05.39
1992	2	11.50
1993	2	17.58
1994	3	00.09
1995	3	06.10
1996	2	12.27
1997	2	18.37
1998	3	00.35
1999	3	06.50
2000	2	13.00
2001	2	19.07
2002	3	01.19
2003	3	07.23
2004	2	13.40
2005	2	19.51
2006	3	01.48
2007	3	08.02
2008	2	14.13
2009	2	20.17
2010	3	02.29

MAGHA

Year	Date	Time
1940	16	01.38
1941	16	07.52
1942	16	13.48
1943	16	20.02
1944	16	02.19
1945	16	08.23
1946	16	14.37
1947	16	20.43
1948	16	02.53
1949	16	09.08
1950	16	15.04
1951	16	21.16
1952	16	03.32
1953	16	09.33
1954	16	15.46
1955	16	21.54
1956	16	04.04
1957	16	10.21
1958	16	16.18
1959	16	22.28
1960	16	04.44
1961	16	10.44
1962	16	16.56
1963	16	23.05
1964	16	05.14
1965	16	11.30
1966	16	17.29
1967	16	23.40
1968	16	06.00
1969	16	12.02
1970	16	18.12
1971	16	00.21
1972	16	06.27
1973	16	12.40
1974	16	18.39
1975	17	00.48
1976	16	07.06
1977	16	13.08
1978	16	19.18
1979	17	01.32
1980	16	07.42
1981	16	13.57
1982	16	19.59
1983	17	02.06
1984	16	08.23
1985	16	14.24
1986	16	20.31
1987	17	02.43
1988	16	08.49
1989	16	15.01
1990	16	21.05
1991	17	03.14
1992	16	09.33
1993	16	15.38
1994	16	21.44
1995	17	03.58
1996	16	10.05
1997	16	16.15
1998	16	22.20
1999	17	04.27
2000	16	10.43
2001	16	16.48
2002	16	22.53
2003	17	05.08
2004	16	11.18
2005	16	17.28
2006	16	23.34
2007	17	05.40
2008	16	11.54
2009	16	17.59
2010	17	00.03

PURVA PHALGUNI

Year	Date	Time
1940	29	21.38
1941	30	03.44
1942	30	09.49
1943	30	15.58
1944	29	22.12
1945	30	04.23
1946	30	10.29
1947	30	16.40
1948	29	22.54
1949	30	04.59
1950	30	11.04
1951	30	17.15
1952	29	23.25
1953	30	05.34
1954	30	11.40
1955	30	17.49
1956	30	00.05
1957	30	06.12
1958	30	12.16
1959	30	18.29
1960	30	00.37
1961	30	06.45
1962	30	12.51
1963	30	19.00
1964	30	01.16
1965	30	07.22
1966	30	13.25
1967	30	19.41
1968	30	01.51
1969	30	08.01
1970	30	14.09
1971	30	20.16
1972	30	02.30
1973	30	08.34
1974	30	14.35
1975	30	20.51
1976	30	02.59
1977	30	09.06
1978	30	15.17
1979	30	21.24
1980	30	03.42
1981	30	09.52
1982	30	15.54
1983	30	22.09
1984	30	04.17
1985	30	10.21
1986	30	16.32
1987	30	22.37
1988	30	04.50
1989	30	10.59
1990	30	16.58
1991	30	23.16
1992	30	05.27
1993	30	11.32
1994	30	17.46
1995	30	23.52
1996	30	06.05
1997	30	12.15
1998	30	18.13
1999	31	00.31
2000	30	06.40
2001	30	12.42
2002	30	18.55
2003	31	01.02
2004	30	07.15
2005	30	13.28
2006	30	19.26
2007	31	01.42
2008	30	07.53
2009	30	13.52
2010	30	20.06

UTTARA PHALGUNI

Year	Date	Time
1940	12	15.25
1941	12	21.39
1942	13	03.36
1943	13	09.48
1944	12	16.05
1945	12	22.06
1946	13	04.21
1947	13	10.32
1948	12	16.40
1949	12	22.55
1950	13	04.53
1951	13	11.04
1952	12	17.22
1953	12	23.20
1954	13	05.31
1955	13	11.42
1956	12	17.49
1957	13	00.06
1958	13	06.06
1959	13	12.17
1960	12	18.34
1961	13	00.32
1962	13	06.41

(continued)

Year	Date	Time
1963	13	12.56
1964	12	19.02
1965	13	01.16
1966	13	07.17
1967	13	13.27
1968	12	19.46
1969	13	01.48
1970	13	07.58
1971	13	14.13
1972	12	20.17
1973	13	02.27
1974	13	08.29
1975	13	14.37
1976	12	20.55
1977	13	02.56
1978	13	09.03
1979	13	15.21
1980	12	21.28
1981	13	03.42
1982	13	09.49
1983	13	15.56
1984	12	22.12
1985	13	04.13
1986	13	10.18
1987	13	16.34
1988	12	22.40
1989	13	04.48
1990	13	10.54
1991	13	17.02
1992	12	23.19
1993	13	05.25
1994	13	11.32
1995	13	17.49
1996	12	23.55
1997	13	06.03
1998	13	12.10
1999	13	18.19
2000	13	00.32
2001	13	06.37
2002	13	12.41
2003	13	18.57
2004	13	01.07
2005	13	07.14
2006	13	13.24
2007	13	19.32
2008	13	01.44
2009	13	07.48
2010	13	13.52

HASTA

Year	Date	Time
1940	26	06.58
1941	26	13.02
1942	26	19.07
1943	27	01.18
1944	26	07.28
1945	26	13.37
1946	26	19.46
1947	27	01.59
1948	26	08.13
1949	26	14.18
1950	26	20.22
1951	27	02.36
1952	26	08.45
1953	26	14.52
1954	26	20.59
1955	27	03.07
1956	26	09.22
1957	26	15.29
1958	26	21.34
1959	27	03.50
1960	26	09.58
1961	26	16.03
1962	26	22.11
1963	27	04.10
1964	26	10.35
1965	26	16.42
1966	26	22.44
1967	27	05.00
1968	26	11.09
1969	26	17.17
1970	26	23.29
1971	27	05.37
1972	26	11.50
1973	26	17.55
1974	26	23.56
1975	27	06.12
1976	26	12.21
1977	26	18.24
1978	27	00.36
1979	27	06.45
1980	26	12.59
1981	26	19.10
1982	27	01.13
1983	27	07.31
1984	26	13.40
1985	26	19.40
1986	27	01.53
1987	27	08.00
1988	26	14.10
1989	26	20.21
1990	27	02.19
1991	27	08.36
1992	26	14.47
1993	26	20.49
1994	27	03.06
1995	27	09.16
1996	26	15.25
1997	26	21.36
1998	27	03.35
1999	27	09.52
2000	26	16.03
2001	26	22.02
2002	27	04.15
2003	27	10.25
2004	26	16.33
2005	26	22.48
2006	27	04.50
2007	27	11.04
2008	26	17.17
2009	26	23.13
2010	27	05.27

CHITRA

Year	Date	Time
1940	9	19.50
1941	10	02.04
1942	10	08.05
1943	10	14.13
1944	9	20.30
1945	10	02.30
1946	10	08.43
1947	10	15.00
1948	9	21.05
1949	10	03.19
1950	10	09.21
1951	10	15.30
1952	9	21.48
1953	10	03.47
1954	10	09.56
1955	10	16.11
1956	9	22.14
1957	10	04.38
1958	10	10.34
1959	10	16.43
1960	9	23.01
1961	10	05.00
1962	10	11.07
1963	10	17.24
1964	9	23.29
1965	10	05.41
1966	10	11.47
1967	10	17.54
1968	9	00.10
1969	10	06.14
1970	10	12.23
1971	10	18.42
1972	10	00.45
1973	10	06.53
1974	10	13.00
1975	10	19.06
1976	10	01.22
1977	10	07.25
1978	10	13.31
1979	10	19.48
1980	10	01.54
1981	10	08.05
1982	10	14.17
1983	10	20.25
1984	10	02.40
1985	10	08.42
1986	10	14.47
1987	10	21.04
1988	10	03.10
1989	10	09.16
1990	10	15.25
1991	10	21.32
1992	10	03.45
1993	10	09.52
1994	10	15.59
1995	10	22.18
1996	10	04.26
1997	10	10.31
1998	10	16.41
1999	10	22.50
2000	10	05.01
2001	10	11.07
2002	10	17.11
2003	10	23.26
2004	10	05.35
2005	10	11.41
2006	10	17.54
2007	11	00.04
2008	10	06.13
2009	10	12.19
2010	10	18.23

SWATI

Year	Date	Time
1940	23	06.22
1941	23	12.28
1942	23	18.34
1943	24	00.46
1944	23	06.52
1945	23	12.59
1946	23	19.11
1947	24	01.23
1948	23	07.37
1949	23	13.45
1950	23	19.49
1951	24	02.03
1952	23	08.11
1953	23	14.16
1954	23	20.28
1955	24	02.34
1956	23	08.45
1957	23	14.54
1958	23	20.59
1959	24	03.17
1960	23	09.25
1961	23	15.29
1962	23	21.40
1963	24	03.48
1964	23	10.00
1965	23	16.10
1966	23	22.12
1967	24	04.27
1968	23	10.35
1969	23	16.40
1970	23	22.55
1971	24	05.06
1972	23	11.16
1973	23	17.25
1974	23	23.25
1975	24	05.40
1976	23	11.50
1977	23	17.51
1978	24	00.06
1979	24	06.14
1980	23	12.22
1981	23	18.36
1982	24	00.41
1983	24	06.57
1984	23	13.10
1985	23	19.08
1986	24	01.22
1987	24	07.31
1988	23	13.37
1989	23	19.50
1990	24	01.51
1991	24	08.03
1992	23	14.15
1993	23	20.15
1994	24	02.33
1995	24	08.46
1996	23	14.52
1997	23	21.06
1998	24	03.08
1999	24	09.20
2000	23	15.24
2001	23	21.32
2002	24	03.45
2003	24	09.57
2004	23	15.59
2005	23	22.15
2006	24	04.21
2007	24	10.33
2008	23	16.48
2009	23	22.44
2010	24	04.56

VISHAKHA

Year	Date	Time
1940	5	14.23
1941	5	20.37
1942	6	02.43
1943	6	08.48
1944	5	15.03
1945	5	21.03
1946	6	03.14
1947	6	09.34
1948	5	15.38
1949	5	21.52
1950	6	03.59
1951	6	10.04
1952	5	16.21
1953	5	22.23
1954	6	04.31
1955	6	10.47
1956	5	16.48
1957	5	22.59
1958	6	05.10
1959	6	11.17
1960	5	17.34
1961	5	23.38
1962	6	05.44
1963	6	12.00
1964	5	18.04
1965	6	00.14
1966	6	06.26
1967	6	12.30
1968	5	18.43
1969	6	00.49
1970	6	06.56
1971	6	13.17
1972	5	19.22
1973	6	01.29
1974	6	07.40
1975	5	13.44
1976	5	19.57
1977	6	02.03
1978	6	08.09
1979	6	14.25
1980	5	20.30
1981	6	02.38
1982	6	08.53
1983	6	15.02
1984	5	21.15
1985	5	03.21
1986	6	09.26
1987	6	15.41
1988	5	21.47
1989	6	03.53
1990	6	10.05
1991	6	16.11
1992	5	22.19
1993	6	04.27
1994	6	10.37
1995	5	16.54
1996	5	23.04
1997	6	05.09
1998	6	11.20
1999	6	17.29
2000	5	23.37
2001	6	05.46
2002	6	11.52
2003	6	18.03
2004	6	00.11
2005	6	06.18
2006	6	12.31
2007	6	18.44
2008	6	00.52
2009	6	06.58
2010	6	13.05

ANURADHA

Year	Date	Time
1940	18	20.26
1941	19	02.35
1942	19	08.42
1943	19	14.53
1944	18	20.59
1945	19	03.03
1946	19	09.18
1947	19	15.28
1948	18	21.40
1949	19	03.52
1950	19	09.57
1951	19	16.09
1952	18	22.18
1953	19	04.22
1954	19	10.37
1955	19	16.43
1956	18	22.49
1957	19	05.00
1958	19	11.05
1959	19	17.21
1960	18	23.33
1961	19	05.36
1962	19	11.51
1963	19	17.58
1964	19	00.05
1965	19	06.19
1966	19	12.23
1967	19	18.34
1968	19	00.44
1969	19	06.45
1970	19	13.02
1971	19	19.14
1972	19	01.21
1973	19	07.35
1974	19	13.38
1975	19	19.48
1976	19	02.00
1977	19	08.00
1978	19	14.16
1979	19	20.25
1980	19	02.28
1981	19	08.43
1982	19	14.50
1983	19	21.03
1984	19	03.19
1985	19	09.18
1986	19	15.33
1987	19	21.43
1988	19	03.45
1989	19	10.01
1990	19	16.05
1991	19	22.12
1992	19	04.25
1993	19	10.24
1994	19	16.41
1995	19	22.57
1996	19	05.00
1997	19	11.16
1998	19	17.22
1999	19	23.29
2000	19	05.44
2001	19	11.44
2002	19	17.56
2003	20	00.09
2004	19	06.08
2005	19	12.23
2006	19	18.34
2007	20	00.42
2008	19	06.59
2009	19	12.59
2010	19	19.08

JYESHTA

Year	Date	Time
1940	2	00.38
1941	2	06.50
1942	2	13.03
1943	2	19.05
1944	2	01.17
1945	2	07.21
1946	2	13.29
1947	2	19.48
1948	2	01.53
1949	2	08.06
1950	2	14.19
1951	2	20.21
1952	2	02.34
1953	2	08.41
1954	2	14.49
1955	2	21.04
1956	2	03.05
1957	2	09.13
1958	2	15.27
1959	2	21.33
1960	2	03.48
1961	2	09.57
1962	2	16.03
1963	2	22.18
1964	2	04.22
1965	2	10.30
1966	2	16.45
1967	2	22.49
1968	2	04.58
1969	2	11.06
1970	2	17.14
1971	2	23.31
1972	2	05.40
1973	2	11.47
1974	2	18.01
1975	3	00.05
1976	2	06.13
1977	2	12.23
1978	2	18.30
1979	3	00.42
1980	2	06.48
1981	2	12.54
1982	2	19.09
1983	3	01.19
1984	2	07.30
1985	2	13.41
1986	2	19.49
1987	3	01.59
1988	2	08.07
1989	2	14.14
1990	2	20.25
1991	3	02.33
1992	2	08.37
1993	2	14.46
1994	2	20.57
1995	3	03.10
1996	2	09.22
1997	2	15.31
1998	2	21.41
1999	3	03.50
2000	2	09.56
2001	2	16.06
2002	2	22.16
2003	3	04.23
2004	2	10.30
2005	2	16.38
2006	2	22.50
2007	3	05.03
2008	2	11.12
2009	2	17.21
2010	2	23.30

MULA

Year	Date	Time
1940	15	03.38
1941	15	09.51
1942	15	15.58
1943	15	22.08
1944	15	04.15
1945	15	10.17
1946	15	16.33
1947	15	22.42
1948	15	04.51
1949	15	11.08
1950	15	17.14
1951	15	23.24
1952	15	05.34
1953	15	11.36
1954	15	17.53
1955	16	00.00
1956	15	06.03
1957	15	12.16
1958	15	18.21
1959	16	00.33
1960	15	06.48
1961	15	12.52
1962	15	19.08
1963	16	01.17
1964	15	07.18
1965	15	13.35
1966	15	19.42
1967	16	01.49
1968	15	08.00
1969	15	14.01
1970	15	20.16
1971	16	02.30
1972	15	08.34
1973	15	14.52
1974	15	20.59
1975	16	03.03
1976	15	09.17
1977	15	15.18
1978	15	21.33
1979	16	03.45
1980	15	09.43
1981	15	15.58
1982	15	22.08
1983	16	04.15
1984	15	10.33
1985	15	16.37
1986	15	22.50
1987	16	05.02
1988	15	11.01
1989	15	17.17
1990	15	23.27
1991	16	05.29
1992	15	11.42
1993	15	17.44
1994	15	23.55
1995	16	06.13
1996	15	12.16
1997	15	18.33
1998	16	00.45
1999	16	06.45
2000	15	13.00
2001	15	19.05
2002	16	01.14
2003	16	07.29
2004	15	13.26
2005	15	19.39
2006	16	01.54
2007	16	07.57
2008	15	14.15
2009	15	20.22
2010	16	02.28

PURVA ASHADHA

Year	Date	Time
1940	28	05.51
1941	28	12.00
1942	28	18.16
1943	29	00.17
1944	28	06.27
1945	28	12.34
1946	28	18.40
1947	29	00.55
1948	28	07.03
1949	28	13.15
1950	28	19.32
1951	29	01.35
1952	28	07.43
1953	28	13.54
1954	28	20.01
1955	29	02.13
1956	28	08.18
1957	28	14.24
1958	28	20.38
1959	29	02.44
1960	28	08.55
1961	28	15.10
1962	28	21.18
1963	29	03.29
1964	28	09.35
1965	28	15.43
1966	28	21.57
1967	29	04.03
1968	28	10.08
1969	28	16.19
1970	28	22.26
1971	29	04.39
1972	28	10.50
1973	28	17.00
1974	28	23.14
1975	29	05.19
1976	28	11.25
1977	28	17.36
1978	28	23.46
1979	29	05.54
1980	28	12.01
1981	28	18.08
1982	29	00.20
1983	29	06.30
1984	28	12.40
1985	28	18.53
1986	29	01.05
1987	29	07.10
1988	28	13.19
1989	28	19.29
1990	29	01.39
1991	29	07.47
1992	28	13.51
1993	28	19.59
1994	29	02.11
1995	29	08.20
1996	28	14.32
1997	28	20.46
1998	29	02.56
1999	29	09.04
2000	28	15.10
2001	28	21.19
2002	29	03.31
2003	29	09.37
2004	28	15.43
2005	28	21.54
2006	29	04.03
2007	29	10.14
2008	28	16.26
2009	28	22.35
2010	29	04.47

UTTARA ASHADHA

Year	Date	Time
1940	11	01.45
1941	10	07.47
1942	10	14.03
1943	10	20.10
1944	11	02.16
1945	10	08.28
1946	10	14.29
1947	10	20.42
1948	11	02.52
1949	10	08.57
1950	10	15.18
1951	10	21.27
1952	11	03.33
1953	10	09.45
1954	10	15.48
1955	10	22.02
1956	11	04.12
1957	10	10.13
1958	10	16.28
1959	10	22.34
1960	11	04.39
1961	10	10.56
1962	10	17.04
1963	10	23.18
1964	11	05.30
1965	10	11.29
1966	10	17.47
1967	10	23.56
1968	11	05.58
1969	10	12.12
1970	10	18.14
1971	11	00.24
1972	11	06.40
1973	10	12.42
1974	10	19.02
1975	11	01.14
1976	11	07.14
1977	10	13.28
1978	10	19.33
1979	11	01.43
1980	11	07.57
1981	10	13.56
1982	10	20.09
1983	11	02.21
1984	11	08.22
1985	10	14.41
1986	10	20.51
1987	11	03.01
1988	11	09.14
1989	10	15.14
1990	10	21.28
1991	11	03.42
1992	11	09.41
1993	10	15.53
1994	10	21.59
1995	11	04.05
1996	11	10.22
1997	10	16.28
1998	10	22.44
1999	11	05.00
2000	11	10.58
2001	10	17.10
2002	10	23.31
2003	11	05.25
2004	11	11.40
2005	10	17.41
2006	10	23.51
2007	11	06.07
2008	11	12.08
2009	10	18.24
2010	11	00.37

SHRAVANA

Year	Date	Time
1940	24	04.03
1941	23	10.09
1942	23	16.16
1943	23	22.31
1944	24	04.34
1945	23	10.41
1946	23	16.53
1947	23	22.57
1948	24	05.07
1949	23	11.18
1950	23	17.30
1951	23	23.47
1952	24	05.53
1953	23	11.58
1954	23	18.11
1955	24	00.18
1956	24	06.27
1957	23	12.36
1958	23	18.42
1959	24	00.53
1960	24	06.59
1961	23	13.08
1962	23	19.25
1963	24	01.36
1964	24	07.44
1965	23	13.53
1966	23	20.01
1967	24	02.13
1968	24	08.20
1969	23	14.25
1970	23	20.35
1971	24	02.43
1972	24	08.51
1973	23	15.03
1974	23	21.17
1975	24	03.30
1976	24	09.37
1977	23	15.42
1978	23	21.53
1979	24	04.04
1980	24	10.10
1981	23	16.18
1982	23	22.28
1983	24	04.35
1984	24	10.44
1985	23	16.54
1986	23	23.07
1987	24	05.22
1988	24	11.27
1989	23	17.35
1990	23	23.48
1991	24	05.55
1992	24	12.03
1993	23	18.10
1994	24	00.16
1995	24	06.27
1996	24	12.34
1997	23	18.45
1998	24	01.04
1999	24	07.13
2000	24	13.20
2001	23	19.28
2002	24	01.36
2003	24	07.48
2004	24	13.55
2005	23	19.59
2006	24	02.14
2007	24	08.19
2008	24	14.27
2009	23	20.42
2010	24	02.51

DHANISHTA

Year	Date	Time
1940	6	07.13
1941	5	13.14
1942	5	19.31
1943	6	01.39
1944	6	07.41
1945	5	13.56
1946	5	20.00
1947	6	02.08
1948	6	08.19
1949	5	14.22
1950	5	20.42
1951	6	02.56
1952	6	08.58
1953	5	15.13
1954	5	21.18
1955	6	03.27
1956	5	09.39
1957	5	15.41
1958	5	21.55
1959	6	04.04
1960	6	10.03
1961	5	16.21
1962	5	22.32
1963	6	04.42
1964	6	10.58
1965	5	16.58
1966	5	23.12
1967	6	05.25
1968	6	11.24
1969	5	17.38
1970	5	23.46
1971	6	05.48
1972	6	12.04
1973	5	18.08
1974	6	00.26
1975	6	06.43
1976	6	12.42
1977	5	18.55
1978	6	01.05
1979	6	07.08
1980	6	13.24
1981	5	19.26
1982	6	01.37
1983	6	07.50
1984	6	13.48
1985	5	20.03
1986	6	02.19
1987	6	08.26

Year	Date	Time
1988	6	14.40
1989	5	20.44
1990	6	02.55
1991	6	09.10
1992	6	15.09
1993	5	21.20
1994	6	03.31
1995	6	09.31
1996	6	15.46
1997	5	21.55
1998	6	04.09
1999	6	10.27
2000	6	16.27
2001	5	22.37
2002	6	04.51
2003	6	10.52
2004	6	17.05
2005	5	23.12
2006	6	05.19
2007	6	11.33
2008	6	17.35
2009	5	23.47
2010	6	06.05

SHATABHISHAK

Year	Date	Time
1940	19	11.41
1941	18	17.51
1942	18	23.59
1943	19	06.11
1944	19	12.16
1945	18	18.23
1946	19	00.36
1947	19	06.40
1948	19	12.46
1949	18	18.58
1950	19	01.10
1951	19	07.25
1952	19	13.34
1953	18	19.40
1954	19	01.52
1955	19	07.59
1956	19	14.05
1957	18	20.17
1958	19	02.26
1959	19	08.33
1960	19	14.39
1961	18	20.47
1962	19	03.03
1963	19	09.16
1964	19	15.24
1965	18	21.34
1966	19	03.45
1967	19	09.52
1968	19	16.00
1969	18	22.07
1970	19	04.17
1971	19	10.24
1972	19	16.30
1973	18	22.40
1974	19	04.58
1975	19	11.08
1976	19	17.17
1977	18	23.26
1978	19	05.34
1979	19	11.44
1980	19	17.50
1981	18	23.59
1982	19	06.12
1983	19	12.16
1984	19	18.22
1985	19	00.34
1986	19	06.46
1987	19	13.00
1988	19	19.07
1989	19	01.15
1990	19	07.30
1991	19	13.36
1992	19	19.42
1993	19	01.53
1994	19	07.59
1995	19	14.06
1996	19	20.14
1997	19	02.23
1998	19	08.44
1999	19	14.53
2000	19	20.59
2001	19	03.11
2002	19	09.17
2003	19	15.25
2004	19	21.36
2005	19	03.40
2006	19	09.55
2007	19	16.01
2008	19	22.04
2009	19	04.22
2010	19	10.31

PURVA BHADRA

Year	Date	Time
1940	3	18.03
1941	4	00.07
1942	4	06.22
1943	4	12.32
1944	3	18.31
1945	4	00.47
1946	4	06.55
1947	4	12.57
1948	3	19.10
1949	4	01.13
1950	4	07.30
1951	4	13.46
1952	3	19.48
1953	4	02.04
1954	4	18.13
1955	4	14.15
1956	3	20.29
1957	4	02.34
1958	4	08.45
1959	4	14.56
1960	3	20.53
1961	4	03.09
1962	4	09.23
1963	4	15.29
1964	3	21.47
1965	4	03.53
1966	4	10.03
1967	4	16.16
1968	3	22.14
1969	4	04.28
1970	4	10.40
1971	4	16.37
1972	3	22.52
1973	4	04.59
1974	4	11.12
1975	4	17.31
1976	3	23.33
1977	4	05.45
1978	4	11.59
1979	4	17.58
1980	4	00.12
1981	4	06.20
1982	4	12.27
1983	4	18.40
1984	4	00.38
1985	4	06.50
1986	4	13.09
1987	4	19.13
1988	4	01.27
1989	4	07.38
1990	4	13.44
1991	4	19.58
1992	4	02.00
1993	4	08.09
1994	4	14.24
1995	4	20.21
1996	4	02.32
1997	4	08.45
1998	4	14.56
1999	4	21.14
2000	4	03.18
2001	4	09.27
2002	4	15.42
2003	4	21.41
2004	4	03.52
2005	4	10.04
2006	4	16.10
2007	4	22.20
2008	4	04.25
2009	4	10.35
2010	4	16.53

UTTARA BHADRA

Year	Date	Time
1940	17	02.26
1941	17	08.40
1942	17	14.50
1943	17	20.57
1944	17	03.04
1945	17	09.12
1946	17	15.25
1947	17	21.29
1948	17	03.33
1949	17	09.46
1950	17	15.58
1951	17	22.09
1952	17	04.20
1953	17	10.30
1954	17	16.41
1955	17	22.47
1956	17	04.52
1957	17	11.04
1958	17	17.16
1959	17	23.20
1960	17	05.26
1961	17	11.36
1962	17	17.48
1963	18	00.00
1964	17	06.10
1965	17	12.22
1966	17	18.35
1967	18	00.39
1968	17	06.46
1969	17	12.57
1970	17	19.05
1971	18	01.10
1972	17	07.17
1973	17	12.25
1974	17	19.43
1975	18	01.52
1976	17	08.02
1977	17	14.16
1978	17	20.23
1979	18	02.30
1980	17	08.38
1981	17	14.46
1982	17	21.00
1983	18	03.03
1984	17	09.07
1985	17	15.21
1986	17	21.31
1987	18	03.42
1988	17	09.53
1989	17	16.02
1990	17	22.17
1991	18	04.22
1992	17	10.26
1993	17	16.42
1994	17	22.47
1995	18	04.51
1996	17	11.01
1997	17	17.08
1998	17	23.26
1999	18	05.38
2000	17	11.43
2001	17	18.00
2002	18	00.05
2003	18	06.08
2004	17	12.21
2005	17	18.26
2006	18	00.40
2007	18	06.47
2008	17	12.48
2009	17	19.07
2010	18	01.16

REVATI

Year	Date	Time
1940	30	13.21
1941	30	19.29
1942	31	01.42
1943	31	07.53
1944	30	13.51
1945	30	20.08
1946	31	02.19
1947	31	08.17
1948	30	14.31
1949	30	20.37
1950	31	02.48
1951	31	09.04
1952	30	15.07
1953	30	21.24
1954	31	03.37
1955	31	09.33
1956	30	15.47
1957	30	21.56
1958	31	04.04
1959	31	10.17
1960	30	16.15
1961	30	22.28
1962	31	04.44
1963	31	10.45
1964	30	17.03
1965	30	23.16
1966	31	05.22
1967	31	11.35
1968	30	17.35
1969	30	23.47
1970	31	06.01
1971	31	11.57
1972	30	18.09
1973	31	00.20
1974	31	06.28
1975	31	12.46
1976	30	18.52
1977	31	01.05
1978	31	07.20
1979	31	13.17
1980	30	19.28
1981	31	01.42
1982	31	07.46
1983	31	13.57
1984	30	19.59
1985	31	02.08
1986	31	08.26
1987	31	14.28
1988	30	20.41
1989	31	02.58
1990	31	09.03
1991	31	15.14
1992	30	21.19
1993	31	03.28
1994	31	09.43
1995	31	15.41
1996	30	21.48
1997	31	04.04
1998	31	10.12
1999	31	16.27
2000	30	22.37
2001	31	04.46
2002	31	11.00
2003	31	16.58
2004	30	23.07
2005	31	05.22
2006	31	11.28
2007	31	17.36
2008	30	23.43
2009	31	05.52
2010	31	12.07

If the year you were born in is not shown here and you wish to find out your cusp details then please visit the following website: www.komilla.com

Bibliography:
Biharim, Bepin, *Myths and Symbols of Vedic Astrology* (Passage Press, USA). Now out of print.
Shubhakaran, K .T., *Nakshatra* (Sagar Publications, India)

Picture credits
All illustrations copyright © Emma Garner. Photographs copyright: © Front Jacket Images of India; p.7 Images of India; p.8 Circa Photo Library; p.9 Ann & Bury Peerless; p.10 Circa Photo Library; p.11 Ann & Bury Peerless; p.12 Images of India; p.15 Telegraph Colour Library; p. 17, 128 and 130 Images of India.